MW00527430

A Light Inside

A Light Inside

Jeannie Suk

BOOKHOUSE

Contents

03
Toward Freedom

04
Harvard

Prologue

A Gift of Freedom

I am surprised to be writing this book. Even as I begin, I have to wonder why the life of a thirty-something law professor would merit an autobiography. Why am I writing it?

I came to this book for particular reasons. Three decades after my family immigrated to the United States, my work there in American law and legal education unexpectedly opened to me the opportunity to connect with Korea where I was born. This was because among the possible universities where I might have had the good fortune to teach, Harvard was where I began my scholarly career and gained tenure. I became the first Korean to be appointed to Harvard Law

School's permanent faculty as a tenured professor of law.

Because Harvard occupies a place of such unique symbolic importance in the cultural imagination of the Korean people, news of my appointment led to wide interest in Korea, of a kind that academics do not usually inspire elsewhere. During President Lee Myung-bak's state visit to the U.S. in the fall of 2011, I was summoned to attend several receptions in his honor. Astonishingly, among the hundreds of Korean community members assembled to greet him at the Pierre Hotel in New York, the President, whom I had not met, recognized my face and knew who I was. Young Korean girls with their mothers on Harvard tours have chased me to request autographs as I walked on campus. My mail is graced with touching letters from Koreans of all ages in the U.S., Asia, and Europe.

It was moving for me to understand, at this inflection point in an immigrant's American journey, that though my achievement was not itself unique, it had great meaning to Koreans. The generous publicity and appreciation I have received in Korea are testimony less to my accomplishments than to the values of Korean society, in which an academic can be a source of inspiration and pride. Those values, namely prizing above all excellence in education and learning, have shaped my life.

I am not *sui generis*. My life has not proceeded separately from the cultural practices, world-historical developments, and population movement that shaped the life of Koreans in America. So rather than continue to be embarrassed at undeserved attention, I came to see how my story was not just my own, but one in which Koreans felt invested—because it is connected to them. Writing this book is a way of honoring that connection, and I write it for the Korean reader.

I want to warn the reader that what follows is imperfect as a recital of facts. First, I'm aware that I am recalling many things I experienced as a child, and a child's-eye view may be more akin to impressions than the facts of what happened.

Second, this is my story, yet I wasn't the only one there. I am troubled at the idea of conscripting family and friends, who live their own stories, to be characters in mine just because I've chosen to write it. I am therefore very selective in touching on them, and that has necessarily affected the story I tell. If some important aspects of my life are missing here, that is why.

Finally, this is not the whole story of my life, and I don't claim exhaustiveness. I try to address some questions I am often asked by Korean students about my upbringing and my path. I attempt to capture some of what is salient and meaningful in my own remembrance. The story is filtered of course by the interpretive mind of the adult I have become.

The result is an autobiographical story that attempts to be honest not only about the life that formed me but also about the aspirations and ways of life I embrace that did not spring inexorably from my background and upbringing. I decided to write this book because I am so frequently asked to explain the connection between how I grew up and how I work and live now. Though it will take me a while to explain in this book, I would summarize the principles that emerge as follows: Find work you love to do. Treat work like play. Always try new things and take risks. Reward yourself often with breaks and rest. Cultivate dear friendships and work to keep them. Dedicate yourself in some way small or large to making and creating things. Mentor young people and be mentored. Learn by teaching others. Have fun.

I am a daughter of Korea, a citizen of the United States, and a student of the world of ideas. The immense good fortune

I have enjoyed has been the handiwork of my mother and my father, whose past and continuing efforts to help me are impossible to overstate. They gave me a gift of freedom. Whatever is good about my life is due to them. My thanks first and foremost go there. I know that my parents and sisters may not remember my childhood the same way I do, so I am grateful also for their tolerance of my writing.

Lani Guinier has for years encouraged me to write in the first person. I thank her for her memoir, which I read the summer before I enrolled as a student at Harvard Law School, as well as for her profound presence in my life since then.

My gratitude to Noah Feldman for his belief in me for all of my adult life is beyond what I can express.

My students at Harvard inspire me each day as reminders of the future in which I have great hope.

01

Exile to Immigration

"There are perhaps no days of our childhood we lived so fully as those we believe we left without having lived them, those we spent with a favorite book."

— Marcel Proust

Childhood

My parents' families lived originally in what is now North Korea, my father's in Pyongyang, and my mother's in Gaesung and Wonsan. When my parents were young children during the Korean War, each of their families fled to South Korea. My mother was two and my father was three. It was January 1951.

My father is the eldest son. My mother's two older brothers died before she was born. As the new eldest child, she was given a boy's name, Song Nam, by my great grandmother, as if to compel her to carry the legacy of the dead sons.

My father's family was landowners. They objected to the

communist North Korean state established in 1948. Laborers who worked on the family's land had previously come into their home claiming the authority to force them to leave, on pain of death. The family was driven out of their property and stripped of their possessions. They went to stay with relatives.

When North Korea invaded South Korea and war broke out in 1950, my grandfather openly supported South Korea and triumphantly welcomed the northern advancement of troops under General MacArthur. But several months later the tide turned and those troops were beaten back, as Chinese forces entered on behalf of North Korea, and United Nations forces retreated. My grandparents understood that the family could not remain safely in North Korea under the Communists. They were among the million refugees who fled during the war.

It was a harrowing passage in that famously cold winter. My father's grandmother disappeared during a bombing, in the massive chaos of crowds fleeing on foot. They searched and screamed but she was never found or heard from again. My father's baby sister died of exposure on my grandmother's back. Her frozen body was placed in a heap without a burial, and the rest kept moving.

The family settled in Seoul, exiled from home, relatives, status, and lands they would not see again. Filled with grief, my father's parents created new lives and livelihoods with great difficulty. When their small business faltered, the family went to Pusan to join some relatives who had better luck. But by then my father had passed the entrance exam for Seoul High School and remained in Seoul to pursue his studies. The family rejoined him when he became a medical student at Seoul National University on a scholarship.

Before the war, my mother's family had an import/export business working with foreign companies. Like many Koreans in that era of Japanese Occupation, my mother's parents spoke Japanese fluently as they were educated in schools established by the Japanese. They were no fans of Communism either. Their house too was taken by the North Korean government and used as a government office building. They also knew as war progressed that they were in trouble in North Korea. They too became refugees, fleeing south on a U. S. military ship from Wonsan in the same month that my father's family fled on foot from Pyongyang.

In Seoul, my mother's father built a successful bus transportation business. My mother was the oldest of three

"Dol", with mom, Seoul 1974.

girls and two boys. The family had wealth and comfort, a house full of servants, and foreign goods. My snapshot of this childhood amidst the poverty-stricken life of post-war Korea is of my mother as a girl instructing the family's driver to drop her off several blocks away from school so she could descend the Land Rover away from the eyes of deprived schoolmates.

My grandfather's business went into sudden and catastrophic ruin in the late 1960s by the time my mother was in college. Again they lost everything. My grandfather became a salary man in an unremarkable company, and the family lived modestly. He often went out of his way, coming home from the office, to bring me American treats, pizza and hamburgers, which were not commonplace in Seoul in those days.

My mother wanted to study medicine at Seoul National University but my grandfather forbade her from taking the exam for a co-educational school, and he thought medical school was too difficult and unbecoming for well brought up girls. Pharmacy was a good proxy to satisfy her desire to study medicine, he said. So my mother enrolled as a pharmacy major at Ewha Womans University. Only a few years later, my grandfather permitted my mother's youngest sister, considered the smartest, to attend the co-ed Seoul National University, but on the condition that she major in home economics.

The middle sister, a strong beauty with a sharp wit, is today a professor of dance. She is that super fun aunt who treats you more like a younger sister than a niece. She and I have always had an important bond. You can imagine what my grandfather felt when, as an obsessed teenager, all she wanted to do was dance. Classical ballet was obscure in 1960s Korea. To my grandfather's eye, it was barely a step removed from exotic dancing. It involved a half-dressed girl being lifted, twirled, and handled on stage by a man in questionably revealing tights. Not appropriate for a girl from a good family. He and my grandmother tried everything to block her passionate pursuit of ballet training. My mother brokered a deal between them that settled matters: my aunt would get herself into Ewha, the top women's college, and my grandparents would grudgingly accept her studying ballet there. She became a professional ballerina and then a university professor.

My parents first met as sixth graders in a group of students preparing together with a tutor for middle school entrance exams. Six years later in college, my parents saw each other again at a meeting specifically for introducing male medical students from Seoul National University to female pharmacy

With dad, Seoul 1975.

students from Ewha. As the elected President of his medical school class, my father was so busy organizing that meeting that he didn't have a chance to talk to my mother but they locked eyes there. They married shortly after graduation. They always teased each other about who pursued whom, with each coyly claiming it was the other. This exchange has produced hours of apparent amusement between them.

I was born in 1973, at the hospital where my father was chief resident in internal medicine. My mother was a special assistant to the German CEO of Boeringher Ingelheim Korea Limited, the pharmaceutical company.

I'm told that I was a precocious storyteller. People came from all around the neighborhood to see and hear with their own eyes and ears the two-year-old girl who would hold court for hours, entertaining crowds, improvising folk tales from memory. I have no doubt that this account has been greatly exaggerated by my family, as myths of adored children generally are. There is no question that as the first-born child of two first-born children, I was adored in this family.

My grandfather was alive then but ill, in his last days. He lay stretched out, waking sometimes to sob spectacularly, filling

With dad as he did his military service.(Top)
With dad and sister, Seogwipo Hospital, Jeju Island, 1978.(Bottom)

the small rooms with unspeakable grief, before going quiet again into the luxury of stupor. It seemed to me that he slept to anesthetize the pain of homesickness.

After my grandfather died, we all lived under one roof in a small apartment in Jamsil, me, my younger sister, my parents, my father's mother, my father's two adult sisters, and his teenage brother. The apartment faced onto an expanse across the street, on which would later stand the 1988 Olympic Village.

My grandmother looked after me while my parents went to work. She loved me like crazy. In the folds of her encompassing embrace, I sometimes wondered if I might stop breathing. Her hands were wet from her labors in the kitchen, her apron splattered with fragrant pickling juices. *Kimchee* mingled with tears. She wore it like a salty perfume and released it from her pores.

My mother's power struggles with her mother in law were par for the course. My mother had borne two daughters and no sons, which greatly distressed my grandmother. Eventually my mother would give birth to a third girl, my youngest sister, which of course meant a lifetime of bemused Korean

Sister's second birthday, Jeju Island, 1977.

exclamations over the misfortune of having three daughters.

My father and mother believed rigidly in Western medicine. My mother did not breastfeed me and thought that American-made formula must contain high-tech ingredients that were nutritionally superior to mother's milk. My grandmother occasionally wanted to use traditional Korean medicinal herbs for various ailments. My mother distanced these strongly odorous natural products with horror, like contraband or accoutrements of devil-worship. I still can't smell these herbs without feeling tense.

In the iconography of the family, what all of this meant, according to my mom, was as follows: My mother was modernity, practical discipline, self-control, and resourcefulness. My grandmother was the old ways, the painful past, incurable sadness, and superstition.

I sat in a window looking out at uneven clotheslines of laundry and brown urns of fermented bean paste on balconies all around me. One summer afternoon, I gently leaned back and gripped the windowsill with the sticky backs of my knees. Then as my legs grew tired, I allowed myself to let go and fall through the air.

From the first-story apartment, I landed in suspension atop a rose bush, thorns and petals stuck on my limbs, as lay breathing at the sky. I waited for someone to notice. When nobody came, I extricated myself and brushed the thorns off. Rose petals in my hair were at once fresh and sickly. I went inside and sat in the window again.

I remember through a child's eyes the signs of daily life in a military dictatorship and the struggle for democracy, the meanings of which I didn't understand until I had long departed. I remember the national curfew. The loud alarm of the air alerts during which traffic stopped and people went to underground shelters. Daily observance of the national anthem that required every person to stop in his tracks as it played at the appointed hour. An uncle tear-gassed in student demonstrations. Friends of my father imprisoned as political dissidents. It would be through television and newspapers in America that my parents and I would later observe Korea's transition to democracy and the rapid developments in Korean society that occurred after we departed.

My mother surveyed the situation and determined that we had to go to America to drive us fully into our future. She had already known in her life what it is to be up and to be down several times before she was thirty. She wasn't intimidated by the prospect of leaving what we had and starting again in a new place. She set out to get us there. But my father had to be convinced gradually. He was the eldest son, and leaving his mother and three siblings for a new country did not sit well with him. My mother assured him they would take care of everyone with an ocean in between. But it would take several years to arrange for my father to take the necessary qualifying examinations, secure a job in the United States, and get visas.

In the meantime, my father was a handsome Captain, completing his mandatory military service in Yangpyeong as an army physician. For his medical licensing requirement of six months' work in a rural hospital, we went to live in Seogwipo on the island of Jeju. Each day I waited outside the hospital for my father to finish work. As soon as I saw him emerge, I dashed with wild joy across an enormous field until I was swept in his arms. That was as happy as I could be, as happy as I remember being.

My father had scores of tales that he would attempt to pass off to me as true. He claimed there was a large pig living underneath the communal outhouse of our housing apartment. He claimed there was a nearby island where an

Kindergarten picnic, Seoul.

entire people who did not eat seaweed soup grew two adjacent chins. He claimed we picked up my sister from under a bridge. All untrue.

Family lore also had it that my name, Chi Yong, originated as the protagonist of a novel my father wrote in college but never published. I don't know whether this is true, but I never got to the bottom of it because I wanted so much to be true to the ideal heroine my father imagined.

In Seoul my mother succeeded in securing for me a coveted spot in the fanciest private kindergarten in the city, which happened to be a Catholic school. The kindergarten's campus was nicer than many colleges and had a large swimming pool. The children wore uniforms of little red capes and hats. Most of the children came to school with a car and driver, and I took the bus to school.

My mother worked full time. She was the only mother who did. On days when moms showed up at school for special events or group birthday celebrations, I was the only child standing alone. Sometimes my mom might dash in late during her lunch break and put in an appearance. She was glamorous in her pink wool Jackie Kennedy suit, pillbox hat,

Kindergarten concert, Seoul 1978.(Top)
Kindergarten graduation, Seoul 1978.(Bottom)

and sunglasses. She always dressed my sister and me in exquisite little children's outfits. My mother was different. Therefore I was different. When she lifted and kissed me in front of everyone, I felt she was not my mother but a starlet who had chosen me to play her daughter. I adored her beauty and was proud she had important things to do. It seemed only natural that my mother would not be able to be with me much of the time. But it hurt.

The nuns who ran the kindergarten were fond of corporal punishment, which they meted out daily. I was hit almost every day with a thick wooden ruler, not for being bad, but to induce me to be better. Was it effective? What I know is that as five-year-old children in a school performance we hit our musical and dance pieces like professionals perfectly. Perfectly rehearsed, in tune, in time, on key. My own children's school assemblies at their elite private school in Cambridge are a cacophonous but joyous mess. But that doesn't mean I want anyone going near my children with a ruler.

I attended several months of first grade in Jamsil with sixty silent children in my class. We all lined up for collective vaccinations, and stood in formation for the quasi-militaristic morning exercises in the school's massive yard. I remember the austere picture of President Park Chung-hee at the head of the classroom as we sat in neat rows facing straight ahead. I don't remember what I did that warranted the punishment of having to stand in front of the class with my hands up in the air until I felt my arms would fall off. Every point lower than 100 that each child scored on a test led to a sharp stroke of the switch on the palms of the hands or backs of the legs.

I was supposed to go to a *hagwon* after school to practice math while my mother was at work. I missed her so much. I sometimes walked by myself to the vicinity of the *hagwon* without going inside. I peered into the basement window where diligent children sat with their heads down and their busy pencils. I wondered if my mother would find out I was a truant and decide to stop going to work so she could stay with me. Soon enough my mother did stop working, because we were going to America.

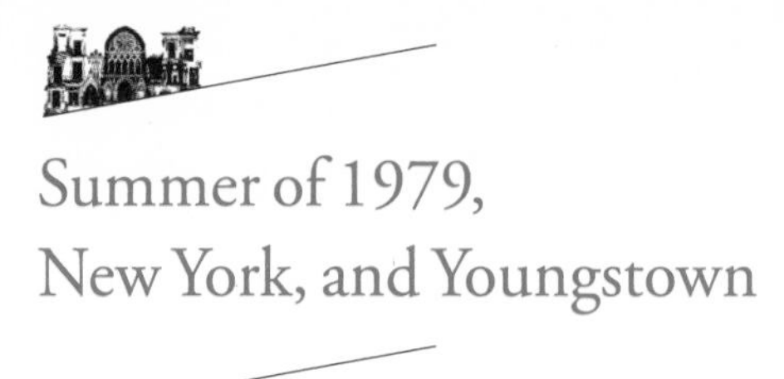

Summer of 1979, New York, and Youngstown

We set off for New York in the summer of 1979. I was six and my sister four. In the past decades, the U. S. had experienced a shortage of physicians in its labor force, as the general U.S. population grew. Congress had passed a law giving immigration preference to highly skilled professionals, and about a third of Korean immigrants in the early 1970s were physicians. Almost half of my father's medical school class immigrated in this wave and now their class reunions sometimes take place in LA or NY rather than Seoul.

I still marvel at the audacity of my parents' decision to leave their home. Barely speaking English and stripped of status, my father started as a medical resident at Brooklyn Jewish

Hospital in New York. Some historians have interpreted the phenomenon of Korean migration to the U.S. in that era as a kind of continuation of Korean War displacement. The experience of leaving what we had and starting in a new place was a repetition. Immigration was both a new future and an exile resonant with a not too far away past.

My aunts later told me that when I left for America my grandmother became desperate, nearly delirious, from missing me. I imagined her wandering through Jamsil weeping and crying out my name, seeing my face in every little girl playing in the street.

I began first grade at Holy Family, a Catholic school in Jamaica, Queens, knowing no English. My parents chose this school not for religious reasons, though my father's mother was Catholic. They chose to pay tuition they could barely afford at this private school rather than send me to the nearby public school that my mother deemed academically inadequate. My parents could afford to send my sister to nursery school only two days a week, and she spent the rest of the week anticipating those precious days.

I am at a loss to describe the utter terror of being thrust

suddenly into a new environment not understanding one word spoken. Language was my connection to the world and the severing of the connection now constituted my disoriented existence. The loneliness of exile from a common language affected everything, even the ability to ask to go to the toilet or get water to drink, let alone to form friendships. In that alienating void, I spent first grade as a mute observer feeling conspicuously non-present and unable to take my place. Each sound from others' lips, laughter in which I could not partake, and activity of the classroom underscored my distance.

At age six, the linguistic brain was plastic. Over seemingly undifferentiated months of desperately passive silence, nonsensical sounds soon became partially recognizable formations that I could eventually grab as pillars to frame what was happening around me. Moving from zero comprehension to hard-won mastery of a situation has perhaps been my painful model for learning and life. In many ways, feeling lost and out of my depth formed(or deformed?) my character. It was a very tough way to give a child an instinct for survival, powers of observation, and what Koreans would call *nunchi*. Nothing since has come remotely close to testing my resilience that way. And despite full linguistic comprehension, I can occasionally still feel those waves of alienation in which I momentarily experience again the sensation of strange uncomprehending disconnection.

When we departed for America, my grandmother gave my sister Chi Hye and me two matching cotton quilts, hers in green and mine in orange. These blankets went with us across halfway around the world and lay on our beds our entire childhoods. We still have them. My sister's is like new, pristine and preserved with no flaws. Mine is a great mess of patches, tattered and nearly destroyed, exhausted from how hard I clung for security and comfort. It has gone with me everywhere I have lived. Over the years it became so impossibly soft and translucent from wear that it now has the consistency of chiffon. I still take out what's left of it from the blanket chest on nights when I need to feel safely wrapped in familiar softness. I try not to though, because each time it disintegrates a bit more and it can't ever be replaced.

When did my problem with *kimchee* surface? By a certain age Korean children are supposed to acquire a taste for *kimchee*, vanquishing whatever infantile revulsion might at first exist. Inevitably a Korean is destined to crave *kimchee*. But this never happened for me. I remained shocked by its knife-sharpness in my nostrils. The unmistakable ferment stifled my breath and made me turn away. I assiduously avoided looking at it, bright orange, immersed in bloody juices, and crammed into the perennial glass jar in the refrigerator where its odor was indelible, inescapable. My mother became less confident that my natural national instinct would kick in any day now. She stopped trying. I began to associate the stinging pickle smell with the shame I felt whenever my perversity was revealed to others: I was a Korean child who could not eat *kimchee*. It was unthinkable.

My mother told me on the Northwest Airlines flight that brought us to America that we were going to a land where people were so prosperous and things so plentiful that nobody even locked their doors against theft. New York in those days was famously unsafe. Our corner of Queens a far cry from the utopia that my mother promised. It seemed that every few weeks something unpleasant and criminal would happen. The window of our brown station wagon parked on the street was smashed with a bat and the cassette player ripped out. Our apartment was robbed, not that we had much to steal.

With her all her newfound time and energy as a stay-at-home mother, my mom made our clothes, learned to cook, and even took jazz improvisation while I had piano lessons. For

Halloween we had her hand-sewn clown costumes made from a wonderful polka-dot fabric. We owned few toys. I remember each one I received at Christmas.

Soon into our first months, my father concluded that New York City was not his American dream, and he wanted to try something else. He had some medical school classmates practicing in Ohio, and he arranged to move there to become a resident at a hospital called Saint Elizabeth, in Youngstown. I was put in a new school there for second grade. Midwestern Youngstown was not exactly a diverse melting pot. I was the only Asian child in the class, and so was my sister. Our English was still in development.

The kindergarten teacher opined that my sister must be deaf, because she didn't respond to questions like other children. My exasperated mother attempted to explain in her own limited English about the process of acquiring a new language. But ultimately it was easier just to send my sister to the hearing specialist for extensive tests, which documented her normal hearing.

My mother had put us in a Catholic school, again because she determined it was the best school available in the area. The religious instruction at the school was something she tolerated but did not seek. Second grade flushed this out because the children were to take their first Communion, so part of each day was devoted to lessons to prepare the children for this sacrament. My mother, however, decided that I would not participate in the Communion-related religious activities. Compounding my alienation from the class due to the language barrier, I alone was now also to sit out during the part of the day that bonded the children together in a common rite of passage. I wondered if it were a conspiracy to emblazon upon me my strangeness, as if I could ever forget.

Youngstown was known for the steel mills that had employed many people in the area. When we arrived in 1980, steel manufacturing had been in decline for the past decade on the way to the shutting down of steel plants and the massive loss of steel sector jobs. Youngstown would never fully recover. My best friend Jennifer's dad was a steelworker who was laid off that year. The air was gloomy.

Later, in law school, I would learn of the famous Korean War-era case involving President Truman's 1952 seizure of the steel mills in order to prevent a steelworker strike that he believed would endanger the war effort in Korea and encourage

Soviet aggression. In *Youngstown Sheet & Tube Company v. Sawyer*, known as the Steel Seizure Case, the Supreme Court ruled that the President lacked legal authority to seize the steel mills. Studying this landmark executive power case in my constitutional law course as a student at Harvard Law School was the first time I connected my childhood sojourn in Youngstown, American military involvement in Korea, and my family's Korean history.

The Koreans in Youngstown were a small but active community. We gathered at a Methodist church each Sunday where we spent all day socializing and eating after the requisite morning religious service. The local television station caught wind of the community's existence and wanted to do a human-interest story on the Koreans in Youngstown and their culture. My mother volunteered me to perform a traditional Korean dance for the television cameras.

"But I don't know how," I said.

"No matter, I'll teach you," she said.

My mother had no idea either, but she put me in a *hanbok*, played a cassette of the tune of "Doraji," and concocted some steps for me that looked good enough to her. The news editor loved the little Korean girl in traditional garb dancing her country's "authentic" dance. I was not only featured on the local news program about Koreans, but a clip of my dance was immortalized as the opening montage for the evening news for years afterward.

When my dancer aunt brought her dancer colleagues to visit us, my mother of course had to show the video of my television moment. They nearly had cardiac arrest from laughing so hard at the random steps my mother had made up willy-nilly. I almost died of embarrassment and vowed that my mother could never direct me into a spotlight again. If I were to embarrass myself, it should be my own doing.

The apartment building where we lived housed the medical residents and was connected to the hospital by a long underground tunnel that looked like a sterile secret bomb shelter. We were allowed to go once each week to the hospital's dining room for dinner as part of my dad's resident privileges.

My parents socialized with two Mexican families in the apartment building. The men were foreign medical graduates who had come to Youngstown like my dad to be residents at the hospital and worked with him there. The three women formed a circle of daytime companions, sharing their sewing and weaving, making pillows and potholders. The men's boasting about the extreme spiciness of their respective cuisines finally came to a head one fateful evening. The Mexicans and the Koreans agreed to face each other in a friendly challenge: *kimchee* against a hot Mexican dish. It was a spice-off.

We didn't stand a chance. My parents' eyes welled with tears while their Mexican friends blithely ate the hottest *kimchee* my mother could produce, without batting an eyelash.

On weekends in Youngstown when we were not at church, there wasn't much to do. We spent a lot of Saturdays wandering about the K-Mart and frolicking in the playground at the local McDonald's. The first time I bit into a Big Mac, I wretched. I had never tasted the quintessentially American pickles, mustard, or mayonnaise before, and in one bite I got all three. I could not figure out what was happening to the familiar taste of hamburger, and I felt sick. I still lose my appetite if I perceive those forbidden condiments in my vicinity, or, heaven help me, if I somehow end up inadvertently ingesting any of them.

Within a few days of starting his residency in Youngstown,

Block Party, Hollis, New York, First residence in America, 1979.

my dad decided it would not work for him there and that we had to get back to New York City. He asked his kind mentor at Brooklyn Jewish Hospital to take him back. So one year after we moved to Ohio, all our stuff went into a U-Haul hitched to our station wagon, including the second-hand synthetic Christmas tree picked up at a garage sale, and the brand new Baldwin upright piano that Santa Claus delivered. We drove to New York, sleeping at rest stops alongside truck drivers on the highway. Once back in Queens, we drove around like nomads, dragging all our worldly possessions behind us, stopping to inquire whenever we saw "For Rent" signs.

The Queens apartment complex where I grew up had an astonishing array of families from the world over. My playmates were from Jordan, Mexico, Armenia, Japan, Czechoslovakia, India, China, Cuba, and Israel. Families from so many different places in the world had such common stories—stories of war, fleeing, displacement, survival, exile, and rebuilding. They had all crossed into a new life in America.

It was a time when children were allowed to roam and play in bands around the neighborhood unaccompanied—before it became a given that parents could not let their children out of their sight unless safely supervised by an adult. Throughout the seasons the neighborhood's children practically lived outside, playing with abandon from morning to dark whenever school was out—skating, biking, tag, hopscotch, jumping rope, running through sprinklers, sledding on plastic.

We stopped in and out of each other's apartments and snacked on leftover dumplings, curry, and goulash. We exchanged tales of Communism, totalitarian dictators, genocide, and torture. We played in each other's traditional garb. We broke limbs and got scraped and bruised, in feuds and heartaches no parents knew. It is mind-boggling from the perspective of the careful surveillance that has become parenting today. My own children will never know the exhilarating dangers of kid-freedom I had as a girl in Queens.

Within two years in America, the language of my thoughts and dreams became English. When this transformation began to show, my parents attempted to establish a rule of speaking Korean at home. But the tide was too strong. My parents' stern resolve softened. As immigrants navigating their new life, they had other pressing worries. Enforcement of parental rules fell aside as the urgent needs of survival took up their energies. I have heard of other Korean immigrant families in which speaking English at home would get a child thrown out or severely punished. But my parents gradually let go the ambition of fully bilingual children and settled for the seamless domestic diglossia that emerged in their place: they continued to speak in Korean and I responded in English.

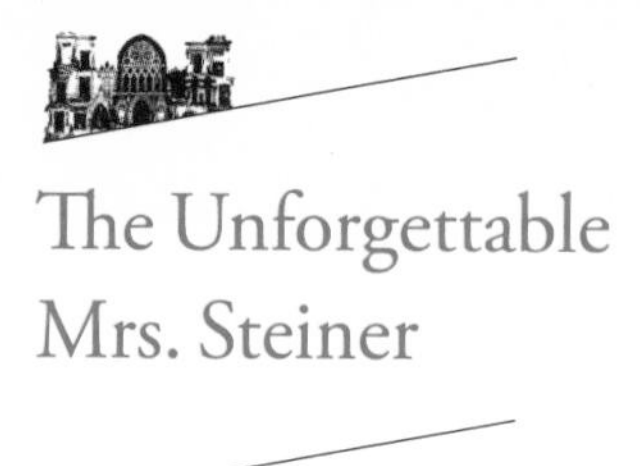

The Unforgettable Mrs. Steiner

At school I was very inhibited. I could now understand and communicate when necessary, but the classroom remained the site of fear and isolation. The gulf was no longer simply linguistic, and it felt even more unbridgeable. The classroom filled me with dread.

At night I had frightful insomnia and half-hallucinations from sleeplessness. Mysteriously, it didn't dawn on me to tell my parents about it, perhaps because I had no idea what I feared. In my unknown and unexplained anxiety, I took to the habit of pulling my hair out, one follicle at a time, and pools of thick black hair amassed underneath my desk at school and next to my bed.

I am not sure when I started having the dream that is my signature childhood dream. Technically it is probably a nightmare. There is a deafening sound of cicadas. I am lost, trying to find the way home. I walk in a field, no, a maze, surrounded by crops taller than me, and I can't see above them. I'm hungry and thirsty. *I'm carrying my sister on my back.* No idea where I am. No sense whether walking takes me farther or closer, or around and around. Nobody to help us, nobody to ask. It is my burden to get us home but there is no end in sight.

Finally waking up from one of these things was like being given new breath. I dreaded confinement inside this dream when I went to sleep. The music of cicadas still sets my teeth on edge, as I discovered in my twenties during long summer nights in Provence.

My elementary school teachers were from a generation when many of the most intelligent and educated women in New York City became life-long public school teachers. Their parents having fled Eastern Europe and become Americans earlier in the twentieth century, these Jewish women were the guides who initiated me. They have passed away by now: Mrs. Klein, Mrs. Newman, Mrs. Rosenthal, Mrs. Steiner, and Mrs. Cohen. With tough and compassionate integrity, each one communicated to me that I could do better than I thought. They were my guardian angels and they didn't let me sink.

I was a mess though. Weeks and months went by at school in a blur. And then my fourth grade teacher, Mrs. Steiner, did something unforgettable. She gave the students an assignment to complete quietly at their desks, and told me to come talk with her outside. I leaned against the hallway wall. She faced me, came in close, confrontational, and exasperated.

"What is wrong?" she asked, "You are every bit as smart as Michelle and Simon and you should be doing just as well."

Michelle and Simon were the two kids in the class who volunteered the right answers all the time. (Incidentally, Simon was a Korean boy whose family soon moved away, and when he became my Facebook friend after almost thirty years of no contact, I learned that he was a Harvard graduate and a physician.) They were always deservingly praised.

"You sit in class like a bump on a log. But you should be one of the best students in the class. Aren't you interested?"

I had nothing to say. I just wept mutely and felt like a bump

At home in Queens, NY 1982.

With my sisters, in Central Park.

on a log.

Mrs. Steiner went home at the end of the day and didn't come back. We learned from the principal that she was ill. She had lung cancer, and within weeks she died.

To commemorate her passing, the principal announced, the school would hold a memorial service at which a student would deliver a eulogy before the whole school. Elementary schools then were very keen on contests. There were contests for everything—spelling bees, science fairs, talent shows. Anyone who wanted to give a speech at Mrs. Steiner's memorial service could enter the contest by reading his or her speech to the principal who would choose the winner.

It did not strike me as odd at the time, pitting in competition children grieving a dead schoolteacher for the privilege of giving her eulogy, like auditioning for a lead in a play. What did occur to me though was that Mrs. Steiner would have respected a child who put herself forward, saying, I can do that, I can throw my hat in the ring, I can stand up before *the entire school* and speak thoughtfully about this difficult topic. Mrs. Steiner would not have respected a bump on a log any more when she was dead than when she was alive. And I imagined that she meant to urge me to put myself forward, not for her sake, but for mine, before she went home to die.

I wrote the eulogy and practiced saying it before going in front of the principal. I put my heart into the speech and tried to sound wise about death. I was not picked. Rosemary, the only other entrant in the contest, was. When I heard her speech, I could see why—it hit all the right heartwarming notes, whereas my attempt was gloomy and pretentious. I didn't get to give the speech. Yet I felt Mrs. Steiner would be proud to see me force myself to try, even while the thought of being at a podium in front of an audience filled me with terror.

After this, I attempted serially to become a champion: of the school spelling bee, the math competition, the talent show, the science fair, and the school theme song contest. I didn't win any of those contests either. I was never the winner but I discovered I liked being in the game. I enjoyed doing what it took to compete and working at producing something to share.

I struggled with debilitating introversion in my daily life at school. But if there was ever a discrete structure that gave explicit permission and a clear avenue to put oneself forward, I found that I wanted to try. It was a mysterious process whereby

Queens Public School, 1983.

one performance at a time I accessed a bit more courage and my unbearable shyness went into suspension for a moment. In a fourth grade play about the American Revolution, I took on the role of Founding Father Patrick Henry, and passionately exclaimed: "Give me liberty or give me death!"

Reading

"A book must be the axe for the frozen sea within us."
— Franz Kafka

My life changed when I was able to read stories and poems. Hans Christian Andersen's *A Little Match Girl* is the first story I remember affecting me deeply. A poor young girl, hungry and barefoot in the snow on a cold New Year's Eve, tries to sell matches on the city streets as passersby ignore her. Freezing, she lights match after match to have a bit of warmth, and in the glow of firelight sees visions of warmth and loveliness—Christmas trees, family feasts, tender holiday joy. She glimpses a shooting star in the sky and recalls her deceased grandmother telling her that meant someone has died and gone to heaven. She basks in the match-light vision of her beloved grandmother who flies with her up toward the skies. In the morning, the girl is found on the street frozen to death and clutching her matches.

When I reflect on why this tale moved me so much, I imagine it might have been because it was about a little girl who was alone and missing the love of her grandmother. I also thought of my grandmother's infant daughter freezing to death on her back during the war. All the little girl has are the matches. The matches seemed to me like little books, bits of light throwing up visions of desire and flights of imagination that shelter her moment by moment from loneliness in a cold and exposed world.

Books became my warmth and refuge. Books in which other people's thoughts and feelings made you think you knew them or they were part of you. I loved knowing I was not the first person for whom this was true, nor would I be the last. Other children separated from me in time and space would have the same solitary journeys as me through books, and in that way I was not alone.

My mother saw my budding love and created a ritual. Every day she picked me up from school, got me a snack at the pizzeria, and took me to the public library across the street for several hours before supper. She sat to read her book and left me to do as I wished.

It was a great adventure to be let loose in there. I opened book after book with a sense of secret, almost naughty, discovery. I devoured the contents of that little Queens library and made it mine. I just couldn't believe an activity that offered such guilty pleasure had parental approval.

Reading was an addiction. Entire summers were spent in delirium reading my way through stacks that I replenished every few days. Brushing my teeth, getting dressed, eating dinner, I was desperate to be reunited with the novel I'd begrudgingly unclasped from my hands. I kept a smuggled light under my bed so I could continue on feverishly long after everyone was asleep. When I injured my arm in a roller-skating accident and it was too painful to move, I demanded that my mother sit still holding a book open in front of my face and turning the pages so I wouldn't have to pause. I loved getting sick with the flu so I could have an excuse to be in bed reading. My mother would bring me warm porridge to have with the books. I admit that today, a ghastly rainy weekend forecast brings me secret hope that I may make a fire in the bedroom and stay curled up reading like a child with no obligations.

My favorite poem was by Wallace Stevens, the American poet who was trained as a lawyer and spent his life working for an insurance company in Connecticut. It tells more about how I survived childhood than almost anything I could describe:

The house was quiet and the world was calm.
The reader became the book; and summer night

Was like the conscious being of the book.
The house was quiet and the world was calm.

The words were spoken as if there was no book,
Except that the reader leaned above the page,

Wanted to lean, wanted much to be
The scholar to whom his book is true, to whom

The summer night is like a perfection of thought.
The house was quiet because it had to be.

The quiet was part of the meaning, part of the mind:
The access of perfection to the page.

And the world was calm. The truth in a calm world,

In which there is no other meaning, itself

Is calm, itself is summer and night, itself
Is the reader leaning late and reading there.[01]

When I finished one book I felt a sinking loss the moment right before the rush of remembering there would be another one, and another one, and infinitely more ahead. The thought of running out of books to read made me anxious. The library imposed a limit to the number of books anyone could borrow at any one time. Sometimes I hid extra library books inside my shirt so I could carry out a few more than my fair share.

I kept a journal in which I wrote down the titles of the books I read along with my brief and quick thoughts about them—what I thought of the fiction's plot, characters, and themes. For a brief time I also included in my journal my thoughts about my own life, but one day when my parents read my journal without asking and became angry over the criticisms and complaints I wrote about them, I stopped and never wrote in a journal again. I stuck to reading.

We didn't own books. They were things you borrowed and returned. I would learn when I was older that some of my friends grew up in homes where walls were covered from floor to ceiling in bookshelves containing unimaginably abundant worlds of wonder. It blew my mind. You could surmise the inner lives and aspirations of the people in the house by their books, those whose bindings were ridged from repeated readings, and others that had never been cracked.

The concept that a home could house the books that fed the minds and hearts of its inhabitants overwhelmed me. "So many books," I murmured, startled by yearning for what it must be to live like this. The friend whose family home was the occasion for my gasp said I sounded like Daisy in *The Great Gatsby* when she comes across the bay to Gatsby's house for the first time and cries softly at his vast collection of English shirts, saying she's never seen such beautiful shirts.

My mother and I fought because I wanted to stay in pajamas all day reading, not even getting up to say hello or eat a meal. My mother did not wish me to be a mere bookworm. She wanted her daughters to be "well-rounded."

I was a devotee of Jane Austen novels, especially *Pride and Prejudice*, which I reread and reread. In that world, a young woman who was to be considered "accomplished," according to one exacting character, "must have a thorough knowledge of music, singing, drawing, dancing, and the modern languages, to deserve the word." Mr. Darcy, the male romantic lead, says, "To all this she must yet add something more substantial, in the improvement of her mind by extensive reading."

Performing

Soon enough I would indeed be able to play the piano, dance, paint, and recite poems. I could entertain my parents' guests at our home with instrumental music and song. I could organize other children to put on a play for the grownups' amusement. My sister displayed her numerous pastels and oil paintings, considered very impressive for the work of a youngster. In the Queens drawing room of my child mind, we were elegantly accomplished girls out of Jane Austen's world.

But something even stranger than fancying myself a pre-Victorian upper-class English heroine occurred in that apartment. I was bitten by a performance bug. I remember exactly when it happened. I was playing C. P. E. Bach's *Solfeggieto in C minor* while some parental guests were over, and I was suddenly overtaken by a strange and strong desire. The desire not merely to be a nicely accomplished girl amusing my parents' friends with an after-dinner diversion, but to blow the audience out of the water with stellar virtuosity. That's right, to shock and awe, to move deeply, to rock their world. It hit me with a thud in my chest that I just wasn't strong enough to play with the speed, power, and control that would require. For that, I actually needed to practice a lot. This childhood epiphany was the root of an ambition that frightened me.

My mother located a proper piano teacher a half hour's drive away to replace the gentle and undemanding teacher in the neighborhood. After being turned away three separate times for lack of space in the schedule, my mother twisted Mrs. Lang's arm to agree at least to meet me. I played a Chopin Mazurka for her. I wasn't much good but she agreed to try to make something of me, purely due to my mother's blandishments. My mom apparently had the alarming look of someone who would not give up or go away.

My mother handed me off to Mrs. Lang, a Jewish woman in her sixties whose parents had immigrated from Eastern

Europe to New York. For the privilege of being Mrs. Lang's student, I had to agree to practice several hours a day. She was sternly disappointed if I came to a lesson unprepared. She was scandalized if I showed up chewing gum, or answered her with an indifferent shrug or a "Yeah," rather than a confident "Yes." She expected me to look her directly in the eye when she spoke and to firmly shake her hand goodbye.

Her most basic demand was as follows. I learned each section of a piece of music, broken up into bits of several measures, by beginning with the metronome set on the lowest speed, click, click, click, click. After many, many repetitions there, and only when I could play the phrase at that speed without any trouble, I was to raise the metronome only one tick. The same process would follow, and another tiny tick up, and then another. Many ticks and repetitions later, I would move to another section of the piece and start again on the lowest speed. Only after the entire piece was assimilated like this, measure by measure, section by section, raised up to tick by tick, could I put the whole thing together end to end. By then my hands and fingers did what they were meant to do. I could play freely at breakneck speed if the piece called for it.

The eventual arrival of the sensation that my hands had a

life of their own gave me freedom from them and from the notes themselves—like unlocking a skylight to set a bird in flight. Sometimes the strange sensation of music being produced through me made me feel as if I were possessed. I have wondered if that is the closest I have come to contact with the divine.

Mrs. Lang required that I perform regularly for audiences and in competitions. She believed I would not practice unless that goal were dangling before me, taunting, enticing, and terrifying. I learned Bach Inventions, Mozart Sonatas, Chopin Nocturnes and Waltzes, Schubert Impromptus, and eventually Bach Preludes and Fugues, Beethoven and Schubert Sonatas, Chopin Etudes, and Debussy Preludes. I took each of them to children's piano competitions to which Mrs. Lang sent me over the course of several years.

But I began to have massive stage fright whenever I had to perform. My stomach painfully knotted. I shivered. My fingers froze solid. Wearing gloves for hours beforehand didn't help. I had paralyzing anxiety that I would get onstage, sit down, desperately delay by adjusting the height of the bench while trying to remember the piece I was supposed to play, and draw a blank. I realize that this is a textbook anxiety dream that everyone has in some form, the one from which you wake up in a sweat, relieved that it was just a dream. But the scene has happened to me for real. I have had my brain and my hands freeze onstage and been unable to get past the horrific mental and physical stumbling block I dreaded. I have been unable to retrieve whole sections of music in mid-concert. I have endured the shame of my apparent incompetence in the silence of a stunned audience.

Knowing that I was even slightly under-practiced fed my fear of choking during performance, which then made it likely to happen. For my debilitating nervousness, I developed two imperfect strategies. First, I would try to over-prepare to such a point that if someone were to wake me at three o'clock in the morning and ask me to play, I could do it, half alert. Second, I would try vividly to visualize my metamorphosis into a completely different person in the act of walking onstage. By the time I sat at the piano, I would try to become that person I needed to be: confident, in control, prepared, and ready to throw caution to the wind.

I never completely beat my musical stage fright. But over several years I was able to wrestle it to the ground for moments here and there instead of allowing it to pin me down. Even apart from the infinite well of pleasure that music and the ability to play has given me in my life, if there is one skill I carry from my childhood experience with music, it is the knowledge that I can almost certainly confront any ghost of performance anxiety in any venue and charge ahead.

As a secondary musical pursuit, I also took violin lessons. My mother felt I should have proficiency in a string instrument as well and brought me to Ms. Han, a vivacious Korean violinist who taught me in a basement room at Queens Community College. After a few years of study, I could play through the first violin of the Bach Double Concerto in D Minor's first movement, adequately if workmanlike. I decided that was enough of the violin for me.

02

Growing Pains

"Only through Art can we emerge from ourselves
and know what another person sees."
— Marcel Proust

Self, Family, Community

Parallel to my adventures in music, I attended ballet class once a week at a local dance studio near home. My aunt was a ballet dancer, and my mother believed ballet had nice benefits for a child's grace and posture. The couple who owned and taught at the studio were dancers trained at the School of American Ballet, the official school of the New York City Ballet.

My parents took me to see the New York City Ballet perform *The Nutcracker* at Lincoln Center. We were fifteen minutes late getting to the show because of traffic driving into the city, and my parents' fruitless search for affordable parking. Knowing we wouldn't be allowed in until a break in the music, we rushed up to the nosebleeds where our seats were. On the elevator's speakers, I could hear the orchestra's brisk rendering of the Overture to Tchaikovsky's score. That music still gives me shivers of anticipation, frustration, and yearning—the hurried anxiety of missing something precious underway.

The lean perfection of the dancers, the clean complexity of the steps, breathtaking scenes of childhood fantasy, and beauty of the live spectacle utterly bewitched me. There were many children onstage in the show, and they looked like they were having so much fun. Those children, the playbill said, were students at the School of American Ballet, known as SAB. Any visions of snowflakes and fairies were upstaged by this vital piece of information, which lodged in my brain like a radioactive splinter.

I tore into my Queens public library, needing urgently to find anything I could read about this ballet school where children were trained to dance on a Lincoln Center stage. I found a book titled *A Very Young Dancer*, a story told with black and white photographs, about a girl my own age, a ten-year-old named Stephanie. It documents her days as a student at SAB where she goes to class each day. The dance studios are enormous window-lit rooms lined with barres at three heights and filled with a beautifully austere discipline. The children's bodies are adorably lean and limber, their legs and arms impossibly long. If they do well, they can advance up through the children's divisions for a chance to become dancers at the New York City Ballet one day.

Unbeknownst to me, the book had been a bestseller when published several years before I came to New York. I learned years later that all girls of my generation who danced found the book as captivating as I did, fixated on its photos, and dreamed of attending SAB. The book follows Stephanie as she auditions with her SAB classmates for the children's parts in the company's *Nutcracker* and is selected to star as Marie throughout that *Nutcracker* season. We go behind the scenes with her as she rehearses her part and experiences performance onstage. The head of the company who oversees her rehearsals and even checks her costumes is a man she calls Mr. B.

I recalled my ballet teacher once instructing me by quoting something Mr. B said about extending the foot in front of you so turned out that a champagne glass could balance on the side of the heel. I hadn't paid too much attention. But now here was Mr. B. again. Who was this Mr. B., I had to know. I began to read every book about ballet I could get my hands on.

Well, as I learned, Mr. B. was George Balanchine, the genius who created the New York City Ballet and choreographed the many works the company performed, such as the beloved *Nutcracker*. As a boy in Russia he had trained at the Imperial Ballet School and danced with the Mariinsky Ballet. In Europe in the 1930s, Balanchine met Lincoln Kirstein, a wealthy young Harvard University graduate and son of an American Jewish department store president, who would eventually become one of the most important influences in the arts in America. Kirstein was a visionary who loved classical ballet and dreamed of establishing an American ballet tradition. After seeing Balanchine's ballets, Kirstein sought to convince him to come to America to make a ballet company that Kirstein would help finance with his money and connections.

Balanchine agreed to come, but he is reported to have said, "But first, a school." This was his American dream. With no school to train young dancers properly in ballet technique, there could be no art of American ballet. And so the School of American Ballet was born in 1934.

"But first, a school." I loved that. Exactly fifty years after its utterance, a skinny eleven-year-old Korean immigrant girl in Queens could not get that simple mantra out of her head. I vowed to become a student at Mr. B.'s school. With each free moment I practiced ballet steps using the back of the living room sofa as a barre, leaping, turning, and jumping until my parents yelled to give it a rest.

My youngest sister, the last of three girls, had recently been born. My mother's mother had arrived from Seoul to help my mother at the close of her pregnancy and to wait for arrival of the baby. I came home from school one day to a very grumpy grandmother, and surmised that something bad had happened. My grandmother told me my mother was at the hospital. My heart stopped for a moment. With seemingly genuine and inconsolable disappointment, she said, "Unfortunately that mother of yours had another daughter." No smile, no congratulations, no relief at everyone's good health. The news that I had a new sister was delivered in a tone no different from if she were saying her wayward daughter had run off with good-for-nothing wastrel and would get what was coming to her.

Ever since that time I always had the urge to tell my little sister again and again how adorable she is. She is now an amazing young woman, a beauty filled with life and spunk. My own daughter looks just like her.

For our family, vacation meant piling into the brown Oldsmobile station wagon and driving long distances, to Binghampton, Buffalo, Boston, or Chicago, to visit with my parents' college or high school classmates. Vacations were spent in close quarters with several Korean families for the weekend, always staying up very late—red-faced dads playing cards, smoking, and drinking beer in white undershirts, cheerful moms making a midnight snack of *udon*, and children showing off magic tricks and telling ghost stories after being chastised for running around wildly. Everyone laughing. Fighting sleep while drinking my late-night soup and then being carried off to bed was delicious.

My parents had a robust social life, and belonged to several strong communities in New York, all of them Korean. My mother's best buddies from Ewha had immigrated to the U.S., as had most of my father's closest friends from SNU. They all had children around our ages. Monthly gatherings rotated through each family's home: my father's schoolmates and their families, and my mother's schoolmates and their families. My parents were happy and laughing in the midst of these old friends. The close friendships my parents kept from their youth in the face of immigration to a new country have been inspiring, a model of life rooted, connected, adaptable, and fun.

An important locus of Korean community in America is the Korean church, and that was always true for my parents. When we arrived in New York, my mother wanted to find a Korean church community that would suit us. There were many possible options there, unlike in Youngstown where there was just one. In what I can only describe as church shopping, we went from church to church, Sunday after Sunday, attending services and the social hour after services, so that my parents could take in the feel of various Korean communities that existed in New York.

Eventually where my mother decided she wanted us to settle was in a Korean church in Manhattan led by a highly charismatic evangelical minister with a several thousand-person following. My mother became a very active member of that community, giving her time and labor to its many far-flung activities and projects over many years. Occasionally groups of church members held worship services in our home. My mother strongly nudged my father to become a deacon of the church, and he did so. He valiantly fought drowsiness in any religious service he ever attended. He learned to pray. He may have been a man of science, even a man of golf, but not quite a man of God at least by nature.

With my mother's involvement in the church, I was sent to the church's summer Bible camp. I made friends there but felt inadequate when people around me began to speak in tongues. The Bible teacher thought I asked too many questions, and I was not her favorite. It seemed that my own connection with the divine was not meant to be cultivated directly in that particular setting. It lay elsewhere. I loved the beauty and austerity of a church, its music, rituals, and prayers, perhaps because of my exposure in early years to my grandmother's Catholicism. The evangelical orientation of many Korean church communities, as it turned out, was not the closest match with my own temperament. But the richness of the experience, both spiritually and communally, for many Koreans in America of which my family is no exception, was very real.

Sunday after church was family time. We had a custom of always going together with friends to the same Korean restaurant, starting from the days when there were really just a couple of establishments on the entire island of Manhattan. They are of course countless now, not to mention the expansion of the Korean reach in Queens, beyond Flushing throughout the 1980s and 1990s, evidenced in the ever amending stretch of businesses with Korean-language signs out Northern Boulevard which leads all the way to Long Island. It always pleased me to imagine that this very in-between expanse was the one crossed by Gatsby, Daisy, Tom, and Nick driving from East and West Egg into the city.

After eating together—the same meal always, *kalbi* and *seol rong tang*—my family headed without fail, rain or shine, to the big Barnes and Noble flagship store near Union Square, where my father wanted to study up-to-date medical books. The rest of us scattered into our own worlds of fascination for several hours. I could always be found ensconced among the shelves of large photo books of art and dance, and biographies of artists, musicians, and dancers. For us the bookstore was a place of dreams, most definitely not a place to purchase. It floors me that my children expect to leave a bookstore owning several new books to add to their full shelves and I oblige.

After five years in the U. S. my family became American citizens. My sister and I nourished each other with stories we wrote for ourselves. It was as if we knew that stories were moving us into an American future. We were creating ourselves from a fragmented and divided past that we could hardly grasp.

That summer my parents sent us to Korea to a camp for

children and young teens organized by the Korean government. Its purpose was to take back to Korea groups of Korean kids who immigrated to the U. S., for a period of exposure to Korean language and culture, as well as some nationalism-oriented tourism. At the head of the large classroom hung a huge portrait of President Chun Doo-hwan. We were lectured by elderly men who did not appear to relate to us and disapproved of the way we dressed. The gulf was vast. On alternate days we traveled together in large tour buses, accompanied by military men to visit the national sites, including a visit to the Demilitarized Zone. My parents had crossed from the twin Korea just over that chain-link border and that was how I had come to have the existence I had.

My best friend at school was Sonya, a smart and clever Armenian girl whose family had a dry-cleaning store in Queens. Like many immigrants who ran this kind of business, Sonya's parents were highly educated in their home country. I was drawn to Sonya because just underneath her proper and well-brought-up demeanor, she had an explosive creativity and outrageousness. She managed to tell lurid tales of Armenians disemboweled by Turkish soldiers with humor and absurdity. We spent hours lip syncing Michael Jackson and Boy George, and scheming elaborately. She was to be a star and I was her groupie.

Hunter

My teacher Mrs. Rosenthal suggested that I think about where I would go after graduating from elementary school. I assumed I would go on like everyone else to the local middle and high schools nearby. She told me about a special experimental school in Manhattan for "gifted" children. I would have to take an entrance exam to be admitted to Hunter, and a small number would be selected. Mrs. Rosenthal herself had attended the school, back when it was only for girls, as had many of the brightest women of her generation in New York City.

My mother thus began to do her due diligence on Hunter, and she found a Korean *hagwon* in Flushing that was preparing children for the Hunter test, in classes that met several times a week after school. When I began to attend the classes several months before the entrance exam, I discovered that the other children had already been preparing for this exam for the past year.

Of the dozen or so children in the group, I had the lowest practice scores, posted prominently in the hall. I was discouraged but determined to improve. It didn't help that when we had to be picked into teams for math competitions, I was the last kid chosen by the other students for any team. I knew I was not as strong as the other children. But it stung when one very bright boy said in front of everyone, very matter of factly, that if *even Jeannie* could solve a particular math problem, it was definitely not hard enough to present a real challenge to the opposing team.

On the cold winter day of the Hunter test, children with their mothers who came out from all the boroughs of New York formed a line wrapped several times around the city block. Much like onstage in a piano recital, my mother could bring me, but she couldn't do it for me or with me. I was on my own out there.

I knew when I completed the exam—math, verbal, and essay—that I had likely made it. The results came two months later. I was admitted to Hunter, along with more than half the other Korean kids in the class at the Flushing *hagwon*—including the very bright boy who found me lacking. Nobody else from my elementary school passed.

So began my seventh-grade life, commuting by bus each day to Hunter on the Upper East Side of Manhattan. Sitting on a whole city block on Park Avenue and 94th street, the building was a former armory for storing weapons and built with no windows. Students affectionately called Hunter the "brick prison."

For the first years, the school intimidated me and I had no comfort in it. As a whole, the Hunter kids were so many levels brighter than those I had known. They were from all the different boroughs of New York, from very different kinds of backgrounds and families, and we all had little obviously in common with each other to begin with. I was overwhelmed academically and socially.

In addition, it was the first time I was expected in the classroom to *analyze* the texts and matters being taught and to *discuss* my own and other students' reactions and opinions. I didn't feel I had anything to say. It felt again as if everyone were speaking a foreign language I didn't understand, leaving me lost and alienated. A mysterious fog would arrive and install a hazy barrier between my literal comprehension and my connection to what was happening. I would see mouths move and hear sounds but I felt strangely blocked from entering the vitality of the classroom scene.

In my parents' house, children making arguments, having opinions, and attempting to explain themselves was highly undesirable behavior. I had been a naturally verbal youngster who enjoyed talking, and my parents tolerated some of this in the family. But in front of others it was a different story. If I attempted to engage in a discussion where I debated or disagreed with an adult, I was later punished for being disrespectful.

On one occasion, I had had a sharp and heated debate with my parents' dinner guest about the motivations of the characters in *The Sound of Music*, and I had repeatedly volleyed and bantered rather than defer. This had led to a strong parental rebuke when the evening ended. My parents genuinely found such behavior embarrassing as an indication of ill-raised, ill-mannered children of bad character. *Mang shin.* "I am humiliated you are my daughter." Their corrections, undertaken with the best intentions in line with their values, put me in a no-man's land between respectful silence and mute inadequacy.

Loneliness surrounded me like a glass wall. I made friends at Hunter but I found it much easier to retreat to books than to talk to people. Talk was fraught. It could get you in trouble. People could think badly of you and become angry. My shyness and inhibition remained, but forms of nonverbal performance suggested ways out of myself.

School of American Ballet

Dance did not involve talk. That was a relief and a release. I became increasingly interested in what my body could do. Over the past year, I had been quietly hoarding information about SAB. I had an extensive diary filled with pictures of dancers I cut out from newspapers and magazines. I was now in Manhattan each day for school at Hunter. It thrilled me that just across town at Lincoln Center, only a subway and a bus ride away, stood waiting this world where I really belonged. I considered and I schemed. From my *Dance Magazine*, which I read religiously, I learned that SAB's annual audition was to take place in late August.

I dragged my mother to the audition. She was thoroughly

reluctant. Her idea of a gracefully well-rounded daughter did not contemplate the extremity of getting carried away and training as a professional dancer. But she brought me, knowing there was only a small chance I would be admitted anyway. I am sure she hoped I would be turned down so I could get this bug out of my system.

We followed the moms and their daughters walking with stick-straight backs, and tightly pulled-back buns. Each child was handed a card with a number to affix to her leotard with a safety pin—108 was mine and I still have it. Scores of girls who gave the impression of all legs, arms, and necks warmed up doing splits in the hallway, waiting for their number to be called.

My audition was five minutes long. I recognized one of the two elderly ladies evaluating me from pictures I had seen from her glamorous prima ballerina days, and from the movie *The Turning Point*, starring Mikhail Baryshnikov. She was the famous Alexandra Danilova, a former wife of Mr. B. The other was Antonina Tumkovsky, the legendary teacher who taught three generations of SAB students. Neither addressed me but spoke only Russian to each other while frowning and pointing to parts of my body.

They lifted each of my legs as far up and to the side as it would go, and scrutinized my pointed feet. I could have been a piece of meat. Finally I was told to do some simple jumps in first position up and down. That was it. I understood that ascertaining skill or talent was not the point of this audition. These women were solely interested in whether the raw material, the physique, was usable for their purposes: long legs, short torso, hips that rotated outward, arched feet, long neck. The Russian ladies did not smile.

The school called that evening. I picked up the phone silently and with heart thumping out of my chest heard Ms. Gleboff, the director of the school, on the line telling my mother that I would have class at SAB each day after school, and two classes on Fridays.

My parents shook their heads. This was not in their plan. They were sure that so much investment in ballet training was unreasonable for a teenager who was aiming to go to college and needed to focus on academic studies. I didn't have to quit dancing, they said. But SAB was for people who wanted to be professional dancers, so what was the point?

I begged as if my life depended on it. One point finally

managed to budge them. The academic record that colleges would evaluate did not begin until the ninth grade. Fine, they agreed, I could enroll in SAB now but I absolutely had to stop in ninth grade. This was the strictly non-negotiable condition.

I had been given a temporary lifeline. I passed the school day looking toward the clock, impatient for 3:15 to arrive so I could dash for the bus across Central Park and then the subway downtown thirty blocks to 66th Street and Broadway, to change into my practice clothes for class at SAB at 4:00.

The light through the windows of the immense studios I had seen in photographs of Mr. B. rehearsing his dancers was every bit as glorious as I imagined. The air inside was always crisp despite the evocative remnants of sweat and resin. I lined up with the other children at the barre in our blue leotards and pink tights and shoes, warmed up and ready for instruction. I was at SAB!

My teachers were legends: Andrei Kramarevsky, Richard Rapp, and Elise Reiman. All had illustrious careers as dancers in Europe and America long before even my parents were born. All were intimidating yet caring in their own way. Their nurture was in the precious passing of the tradition held in their bodies and minds. The gift would be permanent and indelible. It could be handed down only through daily repetition and correction. Body to body, personal and intimate—even as I doubt the teachers knew our names. Their styles were distinctive and yet the beauty of the method they imparted was so coherent and logical that it felt like the laws of nature. This was the way human bodies were meant to move.

Class lasted ninety minutes, and each was structured the same way, beginning at the barre with demi-plies, moving to the center of room, then adagio and allegro, ending with jumps and finally the reverence—choreographed bows and curtsies, to pay respect to the teacher. The classes were so physically demanding that somewhere in the midst of the allegro, leaping, turning, jumping with speed I thought impossible, I often felt I might collapse from respiratory and muscular failure.

The reason I didn't allow myself to falter was the chance that Mr. B. might slip into the room at that moment to observe our progress. People spoke as if he were just around the corner. Unbeknownst to me, Balanchine had died from Creutzfeldt-Jakob Disease three years before my arrival at SAB. His presence was so powerful that almost a year went by anticipating Mr. B.'s appearance before I realized he was gone.

The strict constraints of classical ballet technique gave untold satisfaction. There was a right way to execute each movement, from the alignment of the leg and arch of the foot to the tilt of the head and curve of the fingers. I thrived under the hawkish attention to each detail of the body's discipline. My leg muscles, hips, and feet always hurt, and a deep soreness from class was just layered over by more the next. Feet bled, toenails blackened and fell away. I developed Achilles tendonitis that flared up for years afterward.

Internalizing the aesthetic logic of ballet's established forms through painstaking repetition produced in me a sensation of the highest high imaginable. Having never tried illegal drugs, I have not experienced a drug high and I don't need to. My life since then took on the character of a quest for the holy grail—the wish to be able to feel that high once again.

I found enormous teen independence in going daily on the bus and subway from Hunter to SAB, and then taking the train home. The city felt like my playground. The New York Public Library for the Performing Arts was where I read all I could on the history of dance, and through recordings learned by heart the classics of the ballet repertoire—Swan Lake, Giselle, Don Quixote, La Bayadere, Romeo and Juliet—in performances by

"Internalizing the aesthetic logic of ballet's established forms through painstaking repetition produced in me a sensation of the highest high imaginable."

At SAB, 1987.

greats like Fonteyn, Nureyev, Makarova, and Baryshnikov.

On weekends occasionally I went to an extra ballet class at the studio of the renowned teacher David Howard, though I was not really supposed to take class outside of SAB. One Saturday, I saw that Baryshnikov was taking the same class, warming up at the barre and then executing the combinations the teacher gave us. It thrilled me that I shared with this extraordinary artist a common language in which we were both continuing students. Not even international stage stardom released the body from its need each day to begin exercises with slow and deliberate demi-plies in first position. Everything rested on the fundamentals, which took so much to attain and retain. Steps could not be skipped.

On winter evenings after ballet class, I stayed behind at Lincoln Center to catch the New York City Ballet perform. At dusk the lights of the theaters—the Metropolitan Opera House, Avery Fisher Hall, and the New York State Theater—illuminated the central fountain where I sat waiting for curtain. The excitement of audiences arriving in anticipation of the moments to which they would be witness was a contagion. If my Queens library was like a cozy home, Lincoln Center was the exquisite chateau of wealthy godparents who graciously welcomed you to make their house yours, and that is exactly what I did. It was *my* Lincoln Center.

I had become fanatically obsessed with Balanchine's ballets since the summer before I auditioned for SAB. I was in Saratoga Springs, New York, at a math camp where my mother had sent me in hopes I would forget about ballet. Math held little interest for me, and I was bored. It happened that the New York City Ballet had its home in Saratoga Springs for the summer. The math camp kids went to see a performance at an outdoor theater. We watched sitting on the grass on a humid summer night.

The opening bars of Tchaikovsky's *Serenade for Strings in C* joined that first vision on the distant stage: seventeen diagonally standing girls in long tulle of white, each looking up at one hand raised to the sky. What followed was so poignant that my chest clenched. Balanchine's first choreographic work in America, *Serenade* was created as a workshop for the very first students of SAB in 1934, and first performed outdoors on a similar summer night at the family home of Edward Warburg, Kirstein's Harvard classmate and SAB co-founder. Ending with each girl's arms and feet arriving in first position ready to dance, the famous opening sequence is an allegory of artistic discipline through class exercises. It has affected forever my feeling for teaching students.

I must have seen nearly all of Balanchine's ballets in these years as a teen Lincoln Center prowler. I idolized the elegant strength and artistry of ballerinas Heather Watts and Suzanne Farrell. *Concerto Barocco* exemplified the stunning aesthetic that shaped me fundamentally. Perhaps it helped that I knew the structure of the music, having played the Bach Double on the violin, though not anticipating what could be further revealed in seeing Balanchine's steps. Strict, clean, and architectural, the ballet's layers of mathematical construction vividly interpret—with minimal faith—the back and forth intertwining joust of the two violin parts, to make what seems simple about the music complex and the complex simple. What is known becomes confoundingly mysterious, and at the same time a startling clarity is thrust upon you. I could watch this ballet infinitely.

I could write this whole book as a tour of my inner life through Balanchine's work. I will mention just two more of the teen loves I never got over. When I saw *The Four Temperaments*, set to music by Hindemith, I felt every bit the shock of the new as its very first audience must have in 1946. The dance confronts you with the most rigorous classicism and the weirdly flawless distortion of classical line. It is relentlessly aggressive in this juxtaposition and does not let you rest. The ballet positively throttled me and forced recognition of my modernism, after which it could not be denied.

Finally, the *pas de deux* in the Adagio movement of Bizet's *Symphony in C* is a spell at twilight, a tender communion with God. How could a mortal contemplate such a work, let alone invent it? It is unreal. Balanchine described the effect of the ballerina in that dance as "the moon gliding across the sky." You can't even cry. You forget you have breath.

I went to the school's audition for *The Nutcracker*. My classmates and I were told with one glance that we were already too tall for those children's parts. It didn't matter. I hung on still alive to every moment of class each day and soaked like a sponge all that my teachers offered. Emily, Becca, and I made a habit of standing adjacent to each other at the barre for the warm up exercises, and eventually we always lined up at the front and center of the room together, the ones the others would watch. I became a strong and confident dancer. Nothing has been more perfect than an arabesque on point I could hold forever or a triple pirouette both anchored and free.

My days at SAB were numbered. I had made an unholy pact with my parents, and I lived that promise like a condemned man anticipating his day to the gallows. Before long, ninth grade was upon me. At the end of each SAB year, every student was evaluated and was either asked to return for the fall and promoted to the next division, or dismissed from the school. Each annual promotion point was a winnowing process in which most were cut loose, but some who managed to hang on and then not be slain by injuries could perhaps, in a few years, dance in the company. In the end, it was only four girls promoted, out of sixteen. I was one of the four. They were placing in my palm a jewel that was not mine.

My pride at being promoted was immediately overtaken by the inevitability of the day of reckoning. Grim reapers, my parents made good on their promise. They firmly reiterated what I already knew: my time had run out.

In the SAB division to which I was now admitted, class would begin in the middle of the day, and it was not possible to attend both the required ballet classes and a regular school day. The discussion was an absolute nonstarter for my parents. They would not entertain any suggestion that compromises might be made regarding attendance of academic classes at Hunter.

The alternative idea of attending a special private school, for children working or training as performers, which could fit schoolwork around ballet, was anathema. This was the end of the line, they said. Take your bow. You are done.

I suffered my heartbreak in private. I didn't talk to my parents about it. Only my friends at SAB cried in empathy. They were overwhelmed with fifteen-year-old terror and pity. They alone could imagine the pain of being blocked from the thing that made one feel most alive and human.

My parents had no problem with my taking ballet class somewhere once or twice a week.

"Be well-rounded," they said.

I made half-hearted attempts to do so but it was too painful to collude in the decline of something so painstakingly acquired that could only remain with the intense, habitual, daily discipline I craved. I found I could not dance as a hobby. I could not be well-rounded. I stopped altogether. I was finished with ballet. Defeated.

Until I was in my thirties I was not able to sit through a

At grandparents' house in Seoul, 1989.

performance at Lincoln Center without tears. What I saw onstage I felt in my body as leaps that soon realized their fate as phantom aches of the soul. I had to leave the theater during intermission to keep myself from unraveling.

My mother took me to Seoul that summer, possibly as a distraction, and talked the principal of Yewon, the prestigious arts middle school, into allowing me to sit in as a visitor for several weeks. Several of her best friends' daughters attended the school. My mother always had such glee when she was in Seoul surrounded by her siblings and friends in a city that had changed so much in her lifetime and yet was really home to her. Her mood was exuberant in ways that rarely surfaced in New York. Seeing her in Seoul I had the sense that had she not left she would be running the country or at least a major company. I felt sad that her adult life was mostly so distant from her context of belonging. When we first came to the U. S. in 1979, even a phone call to family in Korea was a big event, international travel was rare, but of course the increasing ease of communication and travel over the years since then has completely changed that sense of distance.

As my father and each of his friends progressed through their periods of training to establish themselves in private practice, their lives and interests developed and changed together. One by one, as all succeeded, with growing prosperity, each family moved from small apartments to large houses. As the years went on, the monthly gatherings continued. But eventually instead of staying up all night playing cards and drinking, the dads collectively came to feel that they needed to get to bed shortly after dinner so they could play golf in the morning. They all stopped smoking around the same time. My father played golf with Korean friends every Saturday, Sunday after church, and Wednesday afternoon, short of a blizzard. Afterward they all went out to dinner with great merriment, and occasionally to be treated by a friend who scored a hole-in-one.

Lost

My quitting SAB was supposed to be for the great purpose of my attending and excelling in high school. But I was not doing well there. I knew what discipline and hard work were. But the strictures of high school just did not take. I did not manage to do homework. I did not do assigned reading. I did not submit papers on time. I was terribly unprepared for tests.

At night I read only books not assigned at school. During the day I just wanted to sleep and disappear. I routinely lay awake until sunrise reading furtively in my bed, and then passed the days at school like a zombie. I sat in class and tuned all of it out. I had constant fantasies of escape. Regarding anything required at school, I felt paralyzed and could hardly bring myself to do it.

I was reading poems as if in deep secrecy, sometimes even locked inside a bathroom stall at school while cutting class.

> Labour is blossoming or dancing where
> The body is not bruised to pleasure soul.
> Nor beauty born out of its own despair,
> Nor blear-eyed wisdom out of midnight oil.
> O chestnut-tree, great-rooted blossomer,
> Are you the leaf, the blossom or the bole?
> O body swayed to music, O brightening glance,
> How can we know the dancer from the dance? [02]

My mother opened the bag I carried listlessly back and forth from school, and found my well-thumbed Yeats, but also saw that I didn't even keep a notebook for taking notes in class. I just crumpled and stuffed in there whatever papers were handed to me, with little prospect of finding them again. Her distress at my inconsistent grades and general lack of industry provoked her aggression. What was wrong with me? I was lazy. I was worthless. Not even a human being. How could I be her daughter? She could hardly believe I came from her.

My mother had long ago given me a gift of freedom: the library of my childhood. Now it was where I went to try to escape what was required and demanded of me.

I will arise and go now, and go to Innisfree,
And a small cabin build there, of clay and wattles made;
Nine bean-rows will I have there, a hive for the honey-bee,
And live alone in the bee-loud glade.

And I shall have some peace there, for peace comes dropping slow,
Dropping from the veils of the morning to where the cricket sings;
There midnight's all a glimmer, and noon a purple glow,
And evening full of the linnet's wings.

I will arise and go now, for always night and day
I hear lake water lapping with low sounds by the shore;
While I stand on the roadway, or on the pavements grey,
I hear it in the deep heart's core. [03]

Innisfree. Faint sounds of freedom emerged from my reading to try to block out the noise of my own inadequacy. I had a long sojourn in the land of English and American poetry. I adored Yeats, Emily Dickenson, and Wallace Stevens. Predictably, Sylvia Plath was also up there. Her poem "Metaphors":

I'm a riddle in nine syllables,
An elephant, a ponderous house,
A melon strolling on two tendrils.
O red fruit, ivory, fine timbers!
This loaf's big with its yeasty rising.
Money's new-minted in this fat purse.
I'm a means, a stage, a cow in calf.
I've eaten a bag of green apples,
Boarded the train there's no getting off. [04]

The "riddle in nine syllables" was obviously pregnancy. But I turned over in my head the "metaphors" to which the title referred. Nine months: nine lines of nine syllables under a title of nine letters. Was pregnancy like the constraints of poetry? The idea of metaphors that "boarded the train there's no getting off" was alarming. Were metaphors like unruly children that, once created, went speeding forth without the creator's control over them? My mother's inability to stop the train I was on?

Riddles didn't produce answers, just more questions. I pored over Robert Graves's understanding of my confusion.

He is quick, thinking in clear images;
I am slow, thinking in broken images.

He becomes dull, trusting to his clear images;
I become sharp, mistrusting my broken images,

Trusting his images, he assumes their relevance;
Mistrusting my images, I question their relevance.

Assuming their relevance, he assumes the fact,
Questioning their relevance, I question the fact.

When the fact fails him, he questions his senses;
When the fact fails me, I approve my senses.

He continues quick and dull in his clear images;
I continue slow and sharp in my broken images.

He in a new confusion of his understanding;
I in a new understanding of my confusion. [05]

And of course, there were always novels, so many novels. Mary Shelley's *Frankenstein* got precisely my gothic mood of the time. So too Charlotte Bronte's *Jane Eyre*, Emily Bronte's *Wuthering Heights*, and Henry James's, *The Turn of the Screw*. I alternated in identification between the creator Dr. Frankenstein and his creation the monster; or between Jane the soulful heroine of integrity and Bertha the ungovernable shut away somewhere in the grand house. Heathcliffe's dark brooding, and the ambiguous evil of the children looking toward the house made my hair stand on end.

My European history teacher Ms. Kenyon was a young woman everyone admired, with a no-nonsense intelligence, who had left a well-paying job in finance to teach social studies to high schoolers because it was more fulfilling. I was in her class for months, as usual without raising my hand or talking.

After reading a play by Bertolt Brecht about the life of Galileo, I got permission to write my term paper for her class on Galileo, whose story had everything a teenage loner could want: a man's pursuit of the truth, the conflict of science and dogma, heresy and orthodoxy. The truth had such stakes that institutions threatened people with death for saying things the institutions thought untrue. She gave me an A on the paper, but then, worrying me, wanted me to come meet her after class.

I sat silent as Ms. Kenyon focused her laser blue eyes on me and asked how I was capable of writing a paper this good but seemed so lost and unengaged in class. I should be up there with the strongest students, she said. Could I please stop sitting in class like a bump on a log—that again. What was wrong, she wanted to know, was something difficult happening at home? Was I depressed? Overly pressured? She pressed upon me that it didn't matter that I wouldn't get into a prestigious school like Yale. She wanted me to wake up, stop just sitting there, and be interested.

Ms. Kenyon's kick in the pants left me ashamed. I was astonished she thought I could be a good student given how pathetic I felt in class. But I was also horrified that she had noticed me not performing to expectations. Again, I had no answers.

I am slow, thinking in broken images.

I didn't know what was wrong with me. I wanted to disappear.

I will arise and go now, and go to Innisfree…

As the summer approached, my mother thought something needed to change for me. My aimless demeanor was of concern. Perhaps she reconsidered her judgment that I would do well in school if I quit SAB. Obviously now it was too late to go back.

Juilliard

I had continued to play the piano with some but not excessive interest. My sister was attending the Juilliard School's Pre-College program for viola and composition. It was a program for elementary, middle, and high school students consisting of a full day of classes on Saturdays—music theory, solfege, orchestra rehearsal, chorus, master class, and lessons—and requiring several hours of practice at home each day. My mother thought I might be able to make a run at Juilliard's entrance exam at the end of that summer.

I think I was drawn to this idea because Juilliard was in the same building at Lincoln Center as SAB. I didn't know why that mattered but it seemed to me that getting close to the art form of music at high level might enable me to approach ballet again. I knew I could never be a good dancer again. But diving into music study, in spaces contiguous with the dance others were learning in that building, could become some kind of heart-balm if not a substitute.

I began intensive piano studies with Olegna Fuschi. She was a powerful, beautiful, larger than life figure on the Juilliard faculty who taught several children of my mother's acquaintances in the network of Korean doctors' wives in New York. My playing was not nearly as strong as that of her other students and would never be. But again, my mother coaxed her into taking me on.

That summer for the first time I practiced four to six hours each day and met Ms. Fuschi every other day for a lesson. For my Juilliard audition I prepared four pieces: Bach Prelude and Fugue in A Minor, Beethoven Pathetique Sonata, Chopin Etude in A Flat Major, and Debussy Jardins sous la pluie. My playing peaked on the day of the audition. I was presenting as Ms. Fuschi's student, so I am sure the jury looked kindly on me. I was admitted.

Juilliard Pre-College was majority Asian. It was in fact rare

With Ms. Olegna Fuschi, 1990.

to see students of any other ethnicity. Asians ruled there. Some not insignificant number had come from Korea to New York to study at Juilliard, with mothers leaving fathers in Seoul and accompanying their children, with ambitions to nurture the next Midori. Korean American violin student Sarah Chang was then an eight-year-old prodigy, her star already shining brighter than we could imagine. We all understood humility in the face of those blessed by God with a freakish talent that might surface once a generation. But that didn't stymie the earnest love and pursuit of music that surrounded us.

Most others were Asian Americans from Queens, Westchester, Long Island, and New Jersey. They were fantastic musicians most of whom managed to practice four hours after school each day and also be at the top of their academic classes. Those Asian stereotypes were generally true at Juilliard.

What wasn't true was the notion that we didn't have fun. From rehearsals on stages of Lincoln Center to summer music festivals in magical places like Tanglewood and Aspen, the young musicians in their common seriousness created bonds through playfulness and hilarity. Forging relationships though the production of beauty was an exquisite form of friendship.

There was a jolting ethos in the halls of intense aspiration to excellence, the feeling of having determinedly departed base camp for a chance to glimpse the view from the pinnacle. Walking on the practice room floor one was treated to a sound I still carry with me: the layering and melting together of the exercises of phenomenal musicians, ages five to eighteen, working alone in each practice room. What should have produced a clash of winds, strings, and keys created a moving kaleidoscope. But you couldn't listen to such intensity for too long for fear that something might break.

The Korean Juilliard mothers were a formidable cabal. The community was tight, and the information in their circle was the stuff of high intrigue and classified secrets. Many of them brought their children to Juilliard on Saturday morning and simply stayed in the building schmoozing until dark. Parents were not allowed to go in with their children for their classes, but many mothers were fixtures at their children's lessons, taking notes and instructions for monitoring the week's practice sessions. If their children went to sleep-away music camp in the summer, they too moved their lives for that period to the same rural, mountain, or European town, and ensured their children were properly taught, fed, and practiced. The moms were visible and audible spectacles in their own right,

Solo Recital, Juilliard School, New York.

enlivening the Juilliard landscape with their antics as zealous advocates on behalf of their talented children.

My mother did not evince that high level of attention, ambition, or stamina in this realm, however. If she happened to sit in on my lessons, she dozed or read a book while she waited. If you asked her what precise pieces of music I was working on, she would not really have been able to say. She was actually not very interested in monitoring my doings in any detail. Her signature maternal mode was to *bring* me to the opportunity or event, then leave me with the expert and get out of the way. She did not think she knew enough about the situation to exercise any detailed authority. She just put me together with those who did and left it at that. In the high-octane group of Juilliard mothers she had relatively low power or visibility. She kept a consistent presence, but as a junior lunchtime member rather than an all-day committed stalwart.

The sacrifices that many Korean parents made to advance their children's education in music were mind-boggling. The meaning of their lives appeared simply to reduce to their children's education. My mother embodied a mixed message. On the one hand, we were present in that milieu and benefited greatly from proximity to the intensity and excellence of the others. On the other hand, my mother could not help but evince slight disdain for the phenomenon of sacrificing excessively as a parent for the sake of the child. No matter how valuable the pursuit, my mother recoiled at excess. She tried to avoid making her children feel burdened by parental sacrifice. (Even today she always tells me to put her in a nursing home when she gets old and senile instead of taking on the burden of her care.) I never felt she was more invested than I was in my music studies or anything else. She never made me practice either(but if she had, I surely would have developed much better technique).

During my studies at Juilliard, I was supposed to practice four hours at home each day. In reality I was not consistent in my practicing. Sometimes I showed up for my lesson having done nothing. But we all had to perform regularly in master class, in which all students listened to each other perform and heard the teacher's critique. So every piece of music we each worked on led at the very least to that performance goal if not more. If I didn't practice, I would be unprepared for the performance, and that would be highly unpleasant. I really loved being part of this particular form of life, but I knew I was not even close to being among the better musicians at Juilliard.

After Solo Recital, Juilliard School, New York 1990.

"There was a jolting ethos in the halls of intense aspiration to excellence."

Summer was the time to focus every day on music. Ms. Fuschi took her students(along with a handful of Juilliard moms) to Europe. We traveled together for two months in a big bus, stopping in the glorious cities and charming towns of Spain, Italy, and France where we played in concerts nearly every evening. It was an absolutely wondrous way for a motley crew of teenagers and children to see Europe for the first time—delighting in the Mediterranean Sea, the Alps, the Prado, and St. Peter's Cathedral by day, and performing in old concert halls and medieval churches by night. Through these performances, rain or shine, before foreign audiences in myriad venues, the stage fright that had once plagued me retreated and all but disappeared that summer.

Returning to New York, paintings and architecture I saw for the first time in Europe haunted me. I threw myself into my high school art history course. Having hopelessly fallen for Provence, I began to study French language with new interest. The Met, the Guggenheim, and the Museum of Modern Art became my playgrounds too. After school I always tried to sneak in a visit before heading home on the subway.

It was in my final year of high school that I started to connect things that preoccupied me and kept me away from my homework—poetry and novels, art, theater, and music—with what was happening in the classroom. I was not near the top of my class, and my work habits were inconsistent at best. But the teachers who taught me philosophy and literature took an interest as they could see me come alive in those subjects. Like so many young readers and students before me, I was ignited by the experience of first reading Plato, Aristotle, Homer, and Sophocles.

Every graduating senior at Juilliard Pre-College performed a full solo recital in Juilliard's recital hall at Lincoln Center. For my recital, I prepared Bach Prelude and Fugue in D Major, Beethoven Sonata in F Major, Brahms Romance and several Brahms Intermezzi, Chopin Barcarolle(my dreamy favorite), and Ravel Jeux d'eau. The night before the recital, I went to bed and could not fall asleep. 2a.m., 3a.m., 4a.m. It was my traditional insomnia—mind racing, frightful thoughts, half-nightmares. Dawn came without my having had a wink of sleep.

The stage fright that might have posed a challenge that day was completely overshadowed by sleep deprivation. Somehow I made it through the concert. I had a gaffe in the midst of the Beethoven sonata, but I recovered and played the rest of the concert, some parts of it rather well. My friends from Hunter

In front of Piano, 1990.(Top)
Juilliard Graduation, 1991.(Bottom)

were there to celebrate with me afterwards. A few months later I repeated the performance at Carnegie Recital Hall.

My friends in high school were artistic theater obsessives. We worked together in the school theater troupe that produced musical plays. I was the music director and orchestral conductor. My best friends were the theater director and the lead actors. Making things with friends was a complement to lonely pursuits and it mingled the pleasures of work and play. The experience was important as a model of non-solitary, joint work—of friendship, creativity, and collaboration. It was empowering to be recognized by peers as a leader by virtue of a knowledge that emerged from solitary discipline.

I am embarrassed to recall that I threw tantrums and got dictatorial if my friends did not sing and play on key or get the rhythm with the highest precision. I thought that what it meant to lead and have high standards was that I was supposed to be intolerant of imperfection. I was an adolescent. The experience taught me that it was not in fact the most important thing to get things to be perfect. In collaborating, getting it exactly right to my specifications was not the point at all. It was being creative in relation to others and working together to make something meaningful. That's what made it fun.

Applying to Yale

Immediately came college application season. My grades and scores did not put me in the top group at Hunter, but my teachers still encouraged me to try for Yale. They saw in my artistic glimmers and musical pursuits the potential for an application that Yale might like. They suspected that demonstrated creativity, imagination, and discipline would be more important than scores, when push came to shove. I had grave doubts but agreed to try.

My mother gnashed her teeth and tore out her hair as I procrastinated and put off work on my applications until the last day when they absolutely had to be mailed. That night my mother had to rush me to the one post office in New

York City that was open late so I could make the deadline. I managed to send off my hurriedly written essays and a tape of the decent part of my piano recital for good measure. My poor mom probably shaved a few years off her life from the stress of watching me bumble around seemingly unconcerned and barely making it.

To add insult to injury, my teenage appearance wasn't exactly my mother's ideal vision of lady-like prettiness.

"Why haven't you brushed your hair? You look like a madwoman," she said.

"I don't have a brush," I said.

"What's wrong with your skin? It's looks like cauliflower," she said.

"I don't know," I said.

"Why are you wearing those shoes? You look like a bum," she said.

"Leave me alone," I said.

"Have you gained weight?"

Let's just say my mother was full of running commentary on me, and I learned to navigate this discursive obstacle course. To figure out which things to take to heart and which to put aside. It was not easy.

But nothing about my mother's orientation toward me was insubstantial cheap talk. She has always, and to this day, without hesitation, shown through actions her absolute willingness to do whatever it takes to help me in any situation. She will gladly spend ten hours of her own time to save me one hour if it makes my life better or easier. She will fight me vociferously if she believes I am going wrong, but support me if I insist on my path. She will happily take on an onerous burden to relieve mine even a little. She will go to prison to leave me free. My unshakable certainty that all this was true throughout my life formed the bedrock of my profound appreciation not just for my mother, but also for my freedom. She gave me that gift.

I applied early action to Yale knowing that by the numbers my chances were not good. Visiting campus for my interview, I had the sense that it was absurd for me to be applying.

Despite myself I fell in love with the place. I was staying with my mother's friend's daughter who was a freshman. She and her friends glowed with health and energy in her room on Old Campus where they seemed to be having so much fun. They were athletic, musical, witty, and literary. They were clean and unadorned. They clearly took their work seriously but wore the seriousness lightly. They had good friends. I admired them and imagined myself in their lives.

My interviewer in the admissions office was a preppy African American Yale graduate in his thirties. He asked what I was most excited about, what I did in my free time, what aspects of friendship were important to me, and what extracurricular activities I saw myself pursuing in college. He was kind and reassuring, but I choked and became tongue-tied and inarticulate. I heard myself sounding like an idiot. I finished the interview fighting back tears.

I was predictably not admitted to Yale early but rather deferred. I would have to wait a few months to get the news either way. My father came to my room with a compassionate look and told me it was really all right if I didn't get in. He loved me unconditionally.

At Hunter Prom, 1991.

Come spring, I was sleeping late on a Saturday morning when my little sister woke me waving a large envelope in my face. I was admitted. Somehow Yale had seen fit to take me.

I hadn't achieved academically what other classmates had. I had not studied thoroughly or performed well on tests or done homework like others with whom I would be enrolling at Yale. I was saved from my alienation in the classroom and my desperate inwardness by falling in love with books, ideas, and art, which opened the world and would become the foundation of my future. I knew I was blessed with amazing and crazy luck. I was grateful and also severely chastened in the way one can only be upon receiving a gift that is undeserved.

03

Toward Freedom

Somewhere someone is traveling furiously toward you,
At incredible speed, traveling day and night,
Through blizzards and desert heat, across torrents, through narrow passes.
But will he know where to find you,
Recognize you when he sees you,
Give you the thing he has for you?
— John Ashbery [06]

College at Yale

We set out for New Haven, my parents' car packed to the gills with stuff I thought I needed away from home for the first time, stuff that turned out to be unnecessary. My mother saw to it that I had a closet of beautiful clothes—silk dresses and wool jackets—to bring with me, imagining I would at the very least need to dress for dinner. Her image was based on photos of old Ivy League days when Yale students wore blazers and ties. Having never known anyone who had gone there from our world, neither of us realized that at Yale in the 1990s the uniform was worn sweaters, sweatpants, and jeans. I adjusted quickly.

My wonder at the unfamiliar was thoroughly matched by that of my new roommate, who drove to New Haven from Illinois with her mother and siblings. Tricia was from a rural town called Kickapoo, and had in part grown up on a farm chasing cows and amidst cornfields. Her family was Irish-Catholic. In the local church where her mother, a music teacher and former nun, played the organ, I would stand as a bridesmaid in her wedding in fourteen years. She came to Yale wearing her hair in two braids down each shoulder, and a t-shirt that said simply, "I gotta be me." To me she was an exotic Midwesterner. To her I was a New Yorker and her first real Asian friend.

Tricia's heart should be in a museum as a model of what a heart should be. She was always herself and nothing less—open and profound. No walls. We have been closest of friends since the day we met. We shared a bedroom that must have been amusing to enter, the dream of the college office that made roommate matches—my half with modernist art posters and shelves of classical music CDs; her half with sweet penguins and bears, and music by Air Supply and Peter Gabriel to which she quickly converted me.

Our suitemate was Lucy, from high-achieving suburban

Pennsylvania. She was a lively and strong blond with a beach tan who had every talent imaginable. She played the piano and the guitar, sang beautifully, drew well, studied formidably, made friends as easily, and brought rollicking laughter where she went. When I returned to our common room in the evenings, new friends who followed Lucy in sat against the wall listening to her play and sing folk and country tunes for hours.

Lucy made daily college life a celebration, and everyone who encountered her wanted to partake of this life. She gave friends silly nicknames and we took them. Mine was "Bean." Tricia's was "Fish." She taught us to delight in Halloween, Christmas, and Easter with humorous and ironic festivities and decorations. There was no costume contest we couldn't win with Lucy transforming us into her kooky vision. She dressed up in wigs and disguises and played pranks; once I spent an entire day believing her to be a new British prospective student who needed to be shown around campus.

On any Yale evening throughout the seasons, our common room on Old Campus was a wholesome hub for freshmen being ridiculous and philosophical deep into the night. It was a glorious time.

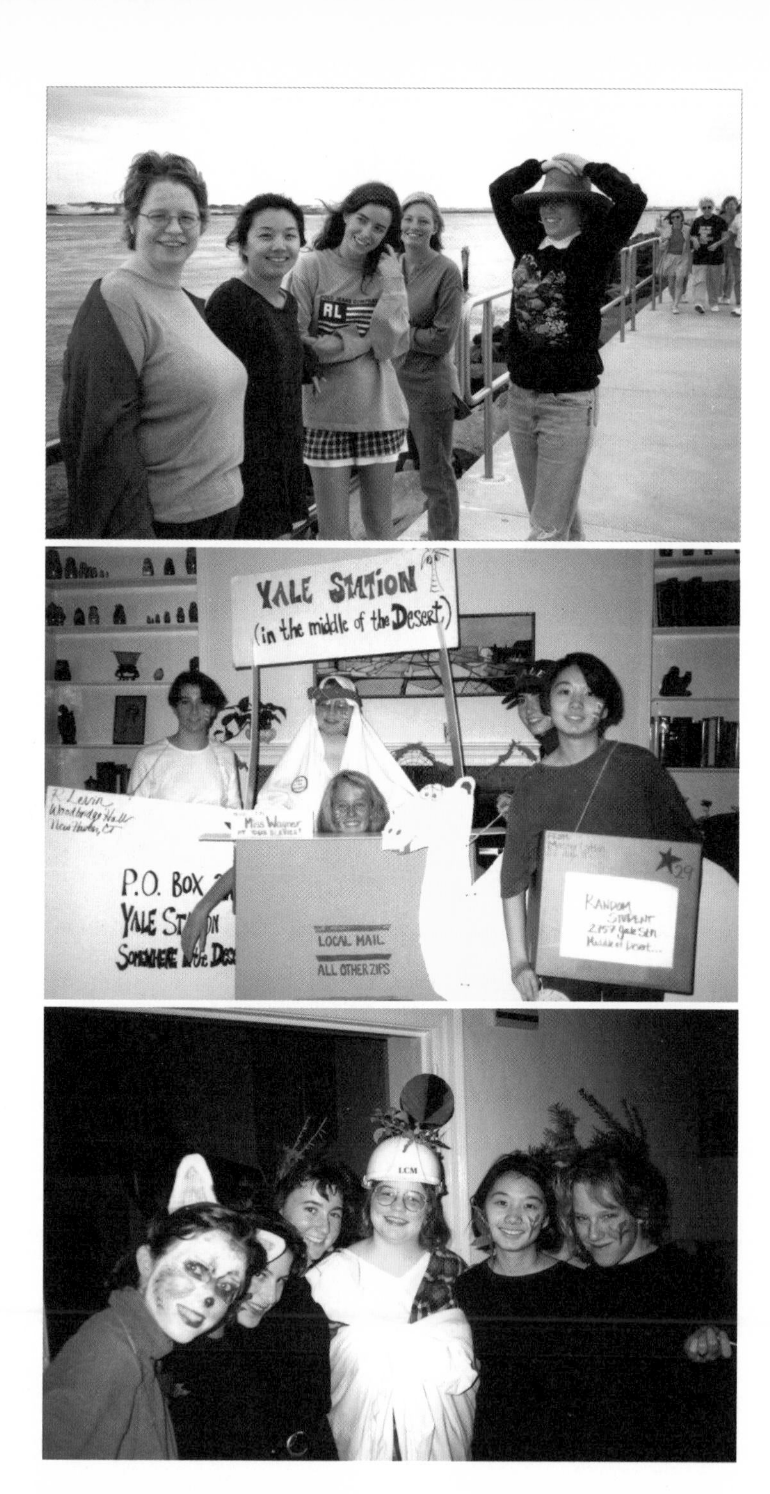

With college roommates, Long Beach Island, New Jersey.(Top)
Halloween Costume Contest at Yale, New Haven CT, 1993 &1994.(Middle, Bottom)

Janna was our fourth. Our nickname for her was "Mama." She was from New Haven, and had attended an urban public school where many students didn't go on to college. She warmly embraced all who came in her orbit. She had no pretensions and was all authenticity, character, and humor. She had had lupus since she was a child. She wore her physical pain lightly and laughed infectiously. When she entered the courtyard of our dormitory, Jonathan Edwards College, everyone heard the reverberation of her ballad against the surrounding stone of gothic buildings. Friends stuck their heads out of the windows and shouted greetings of appreciation. She was easily the most popular person in our class and was simply beloved, even revered.

These friendships were Yale's precious treasures. We have been close through over two decades. We live in different cities now, but each year we set aside time to be together for a long weekend—in Maine, Nantucket, or Connecticut—a tradition we began while in college at Lucy's family's beach house on the New Jersey shore. We talk endlessly, cook, eat, and laugh at anything but mostly at ourselves, sharing the growing pains of getting older. I would not fail to be there.

I adored college. My parents didn't just send me away to

college. They set me free. I could do what I wanted then. They supported me, and unlike many students, I did not have need to take a part-time job to pay my expenses. But they didn't demand to know how I was spending my time, or even what I was studying. It was striking how little they tried to exert control while so strongly supporting me. Whether this was by design, a sign of trust, or a lack of detailed interest, it was a true gift. I felt genuinely free.

I was however still having problems with procrastination and concentration in my classes and frequently neglected the assigned work. I wanted to study philosophy. It was the philosophical questions related to art that grabbed hold of me: What is art? What does it mean for human beings to make things? How do we create meaning through things we make? How do human expression, representation, interpretation work?

The form of making that held fascination was literature. Linguistic discontinuity was so salient in my experience of immigration. I became obsessed with language—how language represents, the relation between words, concepts, and things. The verbal representation of reason and emotion. How it is that language refers to things, but also seems at times to take on its own life? And how does language shape what it means to be human? How does language create personality? Through words we construct the narratives of where we came from, and imagine what our future might be.

I discovered my academic vocation in the study of literary language.

> Much have I travell'd in the realms of gold,
> And many goodly states and kingdoms seen;
> Round many western islands have I been
> Which bards in fealty to Apollo hold.
> Oft of one wide expanse had I been told
> That deep-browed Homer ruled as his demesne;
> Yet did I never breathe its pure serene
> Till I heard Chapman speak out loud and bold:
> Then felt I like some watcher of the skies
> When a new planet swims into his ken;
> Or like stout Cortez when with eagle eyes
> He star'd at the Pacific—and all his men
> Look'd at each other with a wild surmise—
> Silent, upon a peak in Darien.[07]

The epiphany of stunned discovery even among familiar

things was the experience I wanted to have over and over again. It was writing a paper about this Keats poem that hooked me on literary studies at Yale. My poetry professor read the paper I submitted and asked to see me after class. My heart sank—I knew what was coming and was prepared to be abashed.

But it wasn't what I thought. She wanted to see me to tell me I had written a good paper, one that was better than most of what was published in the field. And that my contributions in class were valuable. I was floored. I thought she must have confused me with another student.

The encouragement of a special teacher at the right time when a student is finally ready to hear it can be very powerful. Almost overnight I became a student who paid attention and stayed at the library reading for class. My guilty pleasure in reading late into the night somehow merged that year with the disciplined study of literature. The sensation of discovery got channeled into thinking and writing about texts.

Sometimes people ask me to name the one book from college that affected me. I get nervous answering questions like that because of course there is never just one or even ten. It's the tapestry of all the texts and experiences that comprise the often subterranean thoughts and emotions of a person's inner life. I've tried to give some small snapshots of that process here. But if pushed to name one work that shook me and stayed close, I would have to say *Oedipus Rex*. That play makes its way into my thoughts in some form or another almost every day. Everyone knows the story of Oedipus but it always produces a huge shiver to say it again:

When a king learns from an oracle that his own son will kill him, the father binds his infant son's feet and orders him killed. A servant leaves the infant to die of exposure, but the infant Oedipus is rescued by a shepherd and given to a childless king and queen of a different domain who raise him. The adult Oedipus hears from an oracle that he is destined to kill his father and sleep with his mother. Believing himself to be raised by his true parents, Oedipus leaves their domain to ensure that he not harm them. On the road he encounters his true father, the king who ordered him killed as an infant, and unaware of each other's identities, they fight over the right of way and Oedipus ends up killing his true father. Oedipus then goes on to solve a riddle that frees that kingdom from a curse, and his reward is the kingship and marriage to the queen, his true mother. The dramatic action of the play is the excruciating process whereby Oedipus the King learns bit by bit pieces of information that eventually enable the unbearable truth to be visible: that he has indeed killed his father and married his mother. Oedipus finally gouges out his own eyes, blinding himself.

It is no accident that one of the greatest works of Western literature dramatizes the difficulty of human insight about the self: The idea that, try as you might, you may not know the things about yourself that would be needed to avoid living out precisely the disaster you take pains to prevent. The paradoxical process whereby insights that eventually become visible allow you to piece together a story in which you have had the central role but that also feels out of your control. The unbearableness of the truth, so that you unknowingly avoid it, and then knowing it you wish to blind yourself to it. Insight about the self is elusive, and when it appears, it can be impossible even to look. These struggles are life-long, and it is often when we believe we have everything figured out that we discover the important ways we have been blind.

What I realized toward the end of my undergraduate education was that for years as a teenager I had been blind to how angry and sad I was at the violent loss of my treasured ballet discipline—the thing that had made me feel like myself.

Not having confronted the loss or resolved my pain around it, I had become afraid and unwilling to try anything with true investment. I had been half asleep, anesthetized, and not quite allowing myself to be alive to possibilities. I had been terrified of putting myself on the line and admitting I loved doing something. Investing in excellence and doing what it took to meet high standards had felt dangerous, as I associated it with loss that I couldn't control. It felt safer to do things only halfway and not care so much.

It is mysterious of course how such a block can get unblocked. But I know it had much to do with the luck of having teachers who were willing to commit to me and give me a hard push. Teachers who were able to communicate, simply, "You can do it." And what was vital was the reawakening of desire and allowing myself to feel that to work at learning something was intensely pleasurable. Only late in my years at Yale I began to be open in this way to the opportunities that are a great university's treasures.

The professors who encouraged me in Yale's Literature department were scholars of French literature. I decided to focus my study on French poetry, especially Baudelaire.

La Nature est un temple où de vivants piliers
Laissent parfois sortir de confuses paroles;
L'homme y passe à travers des forêts de symboles
Qui l'observent avec des regards familiers. [08]

Summers studying in France sped up my fluency. My sister and I went to Avignon together and lived in an apartment with enormous windows adjacent to the Palais des Papes. We studied French and francophone literature, made friends, dreamt in French, and loved loved loved Provence. My mother came to join us for the Avignon theater festival. She complained that the plays were in French.

In my final year at Yale, I dared to apply for a Marshall Scholarship, an award that would fully fund graduate study in the United Kingdom for several years. Invited to Washington, D.C. to interview for the prestigious scholarship, I felt that I might very well be unmasked as an empty fraud who knew nothing. I could freeze or stammer and have nothing to say when asked questions. Total humiliation was a distinct possibility.

As I walked through the door to shake hands with the distinguished selection committee, I willed myself once again

Yale Graduation, New Haven, Connecticut, 1995(Top)
《New York Joongang Ilbo》 Dream Tree Award, 1995.(Bottom)

to undergo a transformation in the time it took to walk to the hot seat—a metamorphosis from a sluggish caterpillar into a butterfly. Images of my earlier self walking onstage for a piano recital flashed in my head. The courage it took to sit at a piano in a silent recital hall where you could hear a pin drop, and begin to play as if spontaneously, for discerning ears hearing every nuance—no interview could be as risky and exposed. I breathed and took control. I explained Keats and Baudelaire. I spoke about the relation of literary theorists and philosophers of language. I made jokes that made the interviewers laugh. Really, was this me? I was chosen. I would be given the opportunity to study literature in Oxford on the Marshall Scholarship.

Finishing my final semester at Yale, I met the man I would marry. I was walking briskly from Payne Whitney Gymnasium on a cold New Haven day with wet hair dripping after some laps in the swimming pool. On York Street, out of the corner of my eye, I glimpsed a friend, also named Jeannie, sitting inside a cafe. She was with several of her friends. She and I wordlessly waved to each other through the glass, and I rushed by on the way back to my room.

In a few minutes at home I got a phone call. It was my friend

Jeannie. Her friend Noah had been sitting with her at the café and seen me walk by. We met and fell totally in love. I felt he was nothing short of Byronic. He said he saw us getting old with each other. Being together felt miraculous, as if no human choice could possibly be involved. From the beginning we argued heatedly and constantly, but both of us thought that must be the passion of two greatly matched people in love. In the hubris of youth we didn't realize how much damage we were doing all the while.

Graduate Study in Oxford

In Oxford I enrolled in the Modern Languages department to study French literature. I had the amazing fortune to have as my supervisor Professor Malcolm Bowie, the preeminent scholar of Baudelaire and Proust. He was a princely soul and a writer of erudition and grace I could never hope to be. I had almost no idea what to do around him, and I felt so tongue-tied for the first year of knowing him. But in his heavenly sun-lit study in All Souls College, my reading with him of nineteenth-century French poetry led me to twentieth-century francophone writing that grappled with French literature as a colonial legacy.

J'ai longtemps habité sous de vastes portiques

Que les soleils marins teignaient de mille feux,
Et que leurs grands piliers, droits et majestueux,
Rendaient pareils, le soir, aux grottes basaltiques.

Les houles, en roulant les images des cieux,
Mêlaient d'une façon solennelle et mystique
Les tout-puissants accords de leur riche musique
Aux couleurs du couchant reflété par mes yeux.

C'est là que j'ai vécu dans les voluptés calmes,
Au milieu de l'azur, des vagues, des splendeurs
Et des esclaves nus, tout imprégnés d'odeurs,

Qui me rafraîchissaient le front avec des palmes,
Et dont l'unique soin était d'approfondir
Le secret douloureux qui me faisait languir. [09]

Malcolm assured me I was prepared, and we decided that I would begin work toward a doctoral dissertation on postcolonial literature by French Caribbean writers of African descent. My dissertation would explore the ways in which Caribbean writers engaged, reread, and rewrote the nineteenth-century French literary tradition, working through the themes of crossing, allegory, and trauma to represent problems of reference to the past. I would develop and elaborate insights of postcolonial theory, psychoanalysis, and deconstruction in the French Caribbean literature context.

People I met then would ask me, why are you interested in that? I think they meant it was not obvious why a Korean American student would gravitate to study of that area of world, given that I wasn't French, Caribbean, African, or a colonial subject. I objected then to the notion that a person need justify an intellectual interest by reverting to personal background, identity, and experience. Couldn't texts hold interest in themselves, without reference to autobiography?

I still believe this, but eventually I also came to see that in indirect and non-literal ways, through intellectual work, I may have been exploring some relations and connections to my history. Perhaps my interest in European colonialism had something to do with the Korean experience of Japanese colonialism. Perhaps my fascination with the hybrid linguistic practice of French writers of African descent had something to do with my acquisition of a new language and changing relation to the mother tongue. Perhaps my obsession with the literary representation of home, displacement, and exile by Afro-Caribbean writers had something to do with my experience of displacement from my childhood home and my family's exile from home in North Korea.

My Oxford days were often bleak. During the weeks of term-time, I was routinely not fully over jetlag for an entire term. I would wake up having missed the short sunny part of the morning, and then it would be a cold drizzle all day and begin to go dark in mid-afternoon, just when the day was really starting for me. My mood was as overcast as the Oxford sky. This was such a common affliction for young Americans in Oxford that one of the colleges set up a special lamp that students could sit beneath, to help overcome the deprivation of light that contributed to the poor mood.

But of course I was not immune to the beauty of Oxford's architecture, lawns, and meadows. Walking for hours along the Thames in conversation with friends, passing ancient churches and cemeteries on the way to a simple supper of trout and beer at a pub was heaven. So too were days and days of reading all alone without interruption in the spectacular Duke Humfrey reading room in the Bodleian Library. Surrounded in quiet by those rare and old books, I felt I was in a hallowed place. At dusk, the dons cycling over cobblestones to high table dinner in college with flowing robes half thrown on their shoulders made me content.

At Wadham College, Oxford, England, 1995.

Malcolm found and gently nudged me along when I got lost in the thicket of research. He always seemed to know when rescue was needed. I had awful insomnia related to anxiety about writing. I think it was because I knew my writing couldn't possibly live up to the texts about which I was writing—as if that should have been a goal! When I slept, I dreamt repeatedly about finding the "solution" to my dissertation so that I could capture the formulations that came so clearly in my sleep. But I woke up and all the elaborately and perfectly worked out paragraphs slipped through my fingers and disappeared. I was blocked.

Malcolm, who was a very productive scholar, wrote every day. A mere page and a half each day without fail, no more and no less, he said. Working this way, slowly but surely, a page and a half at a time, in a month he invariably completed a chapter, and in nine months he had a book. He suggested that I too write a bit of my dissertation every day, so that writing would become a mundane habit rather than overblown into huge expectation. I wasn't able to use this advice so much at the time because of my struggles with writer's block. I wrote with such difficulty and in spurts that punctuated the severe blockages. But later in my scholarly life, alas after Malcolm's death, his advice proved to be a godsend. The writer's block I had was essentially performance anxiety, and what Malcolm helped me see was that daily practice was performance. Like practicing one small measure of music with a metronome, click click click. Or painting one tiny square of a canvas at a time.

My first friends in Oxford were two fellow Marshall Scholars, Deborah and Amy, who had each been brilliant undergraduates at Harvard. Deborah was studying history of science, and Amy was learning economics for the first time. We were like the three musketeers—skinny, intense, high-strung American girls running around Oxford, moving so fast toward our futures it made our heads spin. I don't know how I would have made it through without our weekly dinners.

In fifteen years' time, Deborah would be a renowned endocrinologist and research scientist at Massachusetts General Hospital and on the faculty of Harvard Medical School. Amy would be an economics professor at the Massachusetts Institute of Technology; she recently won the Clark Medal, the top American prize for the most promising economist under the age of forty. It is so fun that our distinct professional paths have put us in the same town, at Harvard and MIT. We live within just a few miles of each other now and spend many a weekend day eating in one of our back yards while our children play together.

With parents, Oxford, England, 1996.

My close friend Mira was a Korean American classicist studying Latin poetry. She was a fabulous cook and obsessed with food. I think I was in her room almost every night to sample what she made for dinner and to talk for hours about everything under the sun. Mira was one of a kind—witty, independent, and outspoken. She had powerful opinions and was never a pushover. I was drawn to her because she was so strong and knew exactly what she thought, what she liked and didn't. She was very serious about her studies, and was completely driven by a steadfast hunger for scholarly knowledge. She is now a tenured professor of Classics.

Among my dearest friends to this day, whom I also met in Oxford, are Bert and Mark, both Chinese Americans whose paths were similar to my own. Bert, who was studying Economics as a Marshall Scholar, is a professor at Columbia Law School, and Mark, who was studying Development Economics as a Rhodes Scholar, is my colleague as a professor at Harvard Law School. For the past sixteen years we have supported and helped each other in the closest and most detailed ways through each of the stages of our lives, studies, and careers. We trust each other totally and they are like family to me.

In Oxford I began also to study tae kwon do. My teacher

was an American Rhodes Scholar who was a multiple degree black belt, and he was studying in Oxford as well. He was not Korean. He was so dynamic and charismatic that many of us who had never thought about martial arts before just wanted to follow him where he led us. He taught a whole class of Marshall and Rhodes Scholars tae kwon do in the Oxford gymnasium several times a week, and we loved it. My parents thought it was funny that I had to go all the way to England to learn tae kwon do from a white American Jewish Rhodes Scholar. I made it to brown belt.

In my third year in England, my sister Chi Hye, having graduated from Harvard College, joined me in Oxford as a Marshall Scholar, and lived several blocks from me. I believe we were the first sisters to win the scholarship.

With Malcolm's continual and kind push, and my ever-growing acceptance of imperfection, I finished writing my dissertation in Oxford's libraries inside three years. A few months later, I defended the dissertation and passed the examination. Malcolm sent the manuscript on to Oxford University Press and on his recommendation the press agreed to publish it. I was to return to the U.S. with a doctorate and my first book contract in hand.

Oxford Graduation, Oxford England, 1999.

Yet throughout my work in literary studies, I found myself ill at ease with it. My struggles with writing led me to admit to myself that reading literature gave me pleasure but writing about it did not. I thought that if I pursued a career as a literary scholar, it would always feel awkward, like trying to keep walking in a shoe that didn't fit well. I had tried the monastic academic life and deemed myself lacking the stomach for its core demand—writing. Perhaps I needed to work in a job that wouldn't give me so much anxiety. I felt certain that writing about literature was not what I was meant to do, and that I would always be forcing things if I continued. I felt lost despite objective measures of success—I understood that a doctorate and an Oxford book contract at the age of 26 weren't bad. But still, this path did not feel right.

I felt I had to take a break from writing of abstractions. I had become unconvinced that crafting a better literary interpretation of Baudelaire or Rimbaud would ever make me feel the way I wanted to in my work. I wanted to read Proust's language again and again but I didn't really want to write about it.

I found myself yearning for work that connected ideas and words to practical effects on people and society. I thought law school might be the way. I hungered for consequences. I wanted to feel that the work I did had effects in the world. What was appealing about law at the most basic level was how it affected people's lives concretely. Sometimes it did so as a matter of life and death.

In my youth, images of lawyers were drawn almost exclusively from television and novels. There were no lawyers in my parents' community, and I didn't know any growing up. But when I was an undergraduate at Yale, Harold Koh's name was frequently in the newspapers, for his work as a lawyer for Haitians fleeing violence and persecution after the coup d'etat in 1991. The refugees were being intercepted by the United States, detained at Guantanamo bay, and sent back to Haiti where they would likely be killed. Harold Koh was a Yale Law School professor who, with his students, represented the Haitian refugees in a lawsuit against the United States government in federal court. Like me, he was a Marshall Scholar in Oxford but two decades before. During my time studying there, he returned to spend a research sabbatical in Oxford where I met him. That he was the child of Korean parents who left their homeland and received asylum in the United States after a military coup in their country made his work as a American legal scholar and a lawyer even more inspiring.

With Harold Koh.

Meanwhile, Noah's parents and mine were deeply troubled at the possibility that we might get married—his because I wasn't Jewish, and mine because he wasn't Korean. These reasons were simply stated and perfectly symmetrical. The families were in fact quite similar, each devoted to their own communities, identities, and cultures. Several painful years of tearful struggles amongst each of the families ensued. We decided to marry anyway. We were so in love. It was unclear whether the families would come to celebrate the wedding but they did in the end, in large part because Harold Koh agreed to stand as our *churye*.

At the time Harold was serving in government as Assistant Secretary of State for Democracy, Human Rights, and Labor. He would later become Dean of Yale Law School and then go back in government as Legal Advisor of the State Department. Harold gave a *churye malsum* that moved every person present to tears. He spoke of longstanding hatreds, atrocities, and divisions among national, ethnic, and religious groups that he saw every day in his job. He urged those present to affirm and celebrate moments of pure love whenever they could. He made everyone promise to support our journey together across boundaries we had inherited.

Law at Harvard

I enrolled at Harvard Law School in the fall of 1999. I was hooked from the first day. Being in class made me feel wired with excitement. I couldn't wait to read for class. I couldn't wait to see what would happen in class. I found myself eager to speak in class. What was happening to me? I was far gone, head over heels, no turning back. I unabashedly loved law school and was totally engrossed.

Intellectually, the study of the law fit me in a somewhat unexpected way. It was not obvious why I took so readily to the study of law. I'm not a natural born lawyer. I knew no lawyers growing up, and had almost no exposure to legal ways of thinking before attending law school. Having been deeply immersed in arts and literature previously, I was well primed to appreciate and enjoy the complex texual and performative character of law, and also to enjoy the constraints and discipline of the language of the law. I had become skilled through my work in literary studies in the reading and interpretation of texts. To my delight, the first year of law school centered on the reading and interpretation of legal texts—analyzing verbal formulations for their meanings and consequences, their statements and ambiguities, their relations and discontinuities with prior texts and ideas.

I now had access to vast new material for interpretation. It was a new language. What's more, there was no aspect of human life that was not touched by law. No area of human endeavor that did not have a relation to law. Law had its own seemingly hermetic set of preoccupations, but they were profoundly embedded in culture and deeply resonant with ideas and methods of interpretation familiar to a student of the humanities. It was a "eureka" moment. I simply felt I'd found what I was meant to do.

The law school classroom was thrilling. Along with 140 fellow students I sat in a large classroom in Austin Hall where legal education in America came alive. We sat in assigned seats in semi-circular rows surrounding the professor. The professor called on one student at a time and asked questions that began a series of dialogues that had to be engaged in a public and highly exposed way in front of all classmates. My heart beat as fast as my mind buzzed with almost frenetic excitement—it was probably fright and desire in equal measures.

In class at Harvard Law School, I raised my hand and spoke every day. If I felt intimidated or nervous about being wrong in front of classmates, I forced my hand up and then heard my voice sound more and more confident. What could have made me so scared as to retreat into a shell had the opposite effect. I had the sensation of blossoming. When I have wondered why, I have surmised that it is because the law school classroom was so like a theater of performance, with its rituals, rigor, decorum, traditions, and gravitas. I was strangely at home.

I thought of the child, completely alienated in the classroom, unable to understand the language and unable to participate. I thought of my parents' chastisement when I spoke up and challenged grownups' statements and ideas. I thought of my schoolteachers who puzzled at my silence. Reinvention and reincarnation were possible. It happened for me in the law school classroom. For the first time I was truly alive intellectually and comfortable in my skin.

My teachers were legendary and it is an amazing honor for me to serve with them as their colleague today. My torts professor Morton Horwitz was a sixty-year-old intellectual giant who had written some of the most groundbreaking books in American legal history. Six weeks into the first semester, I made an appointment to talk to him in his office hours about some questions I had about the course. I had just taken a seat across his desk when he told me that I was going to be a law professor, and that he would help me. I was taken aback. He asked me to be his research assistant and I immediately agreed.

He was taking a chance on me after only a few weeks of having me in class. I was very nervous I might disappoint him. I was so invested in doing well in his course and impressing him, it was unhealthy. I became severely ill the night before the final exam, and I'm sure it was psychosomatic. When the exam result came, it was indeed a disappointing grade, my worst among all the courses that first semester.

Professor Horwitz called me to his office. He asked what had happened. I felt like a mess all over again. He said he knew the exam grade did not reflect what I was capable of, and that we would continue to work together. His kindness moved me. I consider myself to have been "discovered" by him. I don't know if I would have been able to see myself as a law professor had he not proactively told me that I would be one. Morty is now a great friend. We often go to hear chamber music together in Boston.

During my first year I also applied to be a research assistant to Professor Lani Guinier. She had recently joined the faculty, becoming the first minority woman to be appointed as a tenured professor at Harvard Law School. She became a household name while I was in college when President Clinton nominated her for the job of Assistant Attorney General for Civil Rights and then was pressured by political attacks caricaturing her views to later withdraw her nomination. I knew her life story from reading her memoir, *Lift Every Voice*. When I contacted her to apply for the research assistant position, I said, "I grew up in Queens too!" She hired me and we worked closely together, meeting often for hours at a time. She nourished me by modeling how teaching and the exchange of ideas went in both directions between student and teacher. She was an extraordinary mentor. To this day we continue to talk for hours about law and life.

At the very end of the first year was the Harvard Law Review competition—a seven-day ordeal that would determine the membership of the elite group of around forty students chosen from the class of 560 who would serve as editors of the storied Harvard Law Review dating to 1887. The competition consisted of a grueling week in which one had to write an article about a Supreme Court case, and then edit an article. It was like running a marathon—just after completing the marathon that was the first year of Harvard Law School. I survived the competition and made it on the Law Review. The best thing about it was my close compatriots on the Review who became my great friends.

My Achilles heel was exam-taking. I loved class. My mind was blown open each day by new ways of thinking. But I could not stand law school exams. They did not reflect my sense of how much and how deeply I had learned. I never became excellent at taking exams. (And thank goodness life is not in fact anything like the soulless anonymous competition of a timed blind-graded exam.)

During my second year in law school, my exams caused me to panic. I had prepared well, I thought, but the exams unnerved me and they went very badly. I was completely convinced that I had failed them. I mentally prepared to receive failing or near-failing grades, and began to make plans to find an alternative path in life. I didn't think I could finish my third and final year at law school after such a disaster. I took deep breaths and waited for the bad news. When the envelope came, I opened it with calm resignation. But the grades were an A and an A^{-}. I looked again and blinked. How was it possible? Some guardian angel was looking out for me yet again. I wouldn't have to leave law school.

But I took the brush with scholastic near-disaster to heart. The two teachers who had taught the courses in which the exams almost knocked me out became close mentors and my gratitude toward each of them is still mingled with wonder at the contingency in not failing. One was in a subject that I currently teach at Harvard, Family Law, and the teacher, Janet Halley, is a fount of inspiration for me—always reinventing and regenerating an intellectual life so filled with delight and originality. She gives endlessly to her students, as she has to me.

Writing

My struggle with writing was on the wane. It was more of a steady stammer rather than a block. I had less and less trouble putting words on a page. I suspected it was because I was writing about law, not literature. Literary studies for me had been like trying to look full on at the sun. Focusing the gaze a bit sideways was better. I was not as daunted by legal texts. The aspiration to straightforwardness, precision, and clarity in legal writing was appealing. It gave me a break from the speechlessness I experienced in the face of literary writing, the self-doubt and the demons. Legal writing was more craft than art, more elegance than sublimity. But legal study didn't lack for wonder and intrigue—it was fascinating. I knew it fit me. The way I inhabited its technique, discipline, and dedication put me in mind of the way I was as a student at SAB. My confidence grew.

In a broad sense, my doctoral work in literature had focused on the representation of home and exile. As a law student I continued to think about the concept of home, but in another sense. I became interested in ways the law conceptually distinguishes private and public. And one way this abstract distinction was made real was in the law's treatment of conduct in the private space of the home, as compared to conduct in the public streets. I approached the renowned criminal law scholar Bill Stuntz to supervise my third-year paper on the concept of home in the criminal law of self-defense. It would eventually turn out to be the germ of the book I would later write on the legal concept of home—though of course I didn't know that then.

Bill knew that I wanted to enter academic life like him. One day, sensing my nerves, he stopped our discussion of my paper, and said simply, "You're going to have a great academic career." Bill was a kind and self-deprecating man who constantly denied his own importance and gave others support and encouragement. An example of his absurd but sincere modesty: as my professor, he told me that my accomplishments made him think his own were unimpressive. He often apologized for taking up my time—even when I had requested the meeting to get his feedback on my work.

The advice Bill shared on research and writing is advice I live by and press on my own students. It was his version of what Malcolm told me in Oxford: write regularly without overly high expectations. Begin writing even when you don't know all you should about your subject. Draft words you're unsure about, and completely rewrite them as you learn more. Write, research, read, rewrite, repeat.

Writing was a way to learn, not something that happens only at the end of learning. Heeding this advice hastened the end of my experience of myself as a troubled writer. It meant giving up the wish for divine inspiration as a spur to writing, or of totally accomplished erudition as a precondition of writing. Daring to write was not a claim to know everything. It could be a humble acknowledgement of the imperfect process of learning a little at a time. Bill helped me feel the burden get lighter.

By then the mysterious, chronic, and life-changing back pain that would hurt Bill every waking moment of his last decade was there. His office was strewn with neck braces, canes, and eventually, a wheelchair. He once wrote that living with this chronic pain was "like having an alarm clock taped to your ear with the volume turned up—and you can't turn it down. You can't run from it: the pain goes where you go and stays where you stay." Throughout it Bill gave me and other students so much, and produced the most important and influential works of criminal law scholarship that set the agenda of the field for an entire generation of scholars.

At my graduation from Harvard Law School, my teacher Lani Guinier received the school's annual teaching award as the choice of my graduating class. It was so rewarding to share that moment with her. By then I knew for certain I wanted to be a teacher, and to work with law students who would be awakened to vital reflection on the relation between the questions what makes us human and how to order our society. She whispered in my ear that she hoped to see me to join her as a colleague in the not-so-distant future.

Working

I went off to work as a law clerk for the great Judge Harry T. Edwards on the U. S. Court of Appeals for the D. C. Circuit. In that year, my habits of mind and work became truly solid for the first time. A law clerk's job is to help the judge, by writing memoranda to brief him on the cases he will hear, and then to aid in the research, drafting, and editing of the judicial opinions he will issue. Judge Edwards made clear that he had the highest standards of excellence for his work product and expected nothing less from his law clerks. He also explained this was a learning process.

Gaining Judge Edwards's trust through the daily challenge of meeting expectations and helping assure that what issued from his chambers was of the highest quality was among the most rewarding pedagogical experiences I have had. It was my year as an apprentice to a master craftsman who cared deeply about teaching young people to become true professionals. He became a close mentor, and later one of the closest friends I could have. Judge Edwards's daily example left a permanent trace on me. Any compliment I have ever received about my work should just be redirected toward him. In the time since that year as my boss, he has taken my breath away with how much he has done to look out for me at every turn in my life and career. I would throw myself in front of a train for him if I could.

My good fortune continued in my selection the following year as a law clerk to Justice David Souter, then a Justice on the Supreme Court of the United States. A Supreme Court clerkship is without a doubt the most highly prized job that one can have as a recent law school graduate. A year inside that marble palace, as one of thirty-five young law clerks only one year out of law school, intimately enmeshed in the work of the Supreme Court was a heady experience to say the least. The Court heard several important and high-profile cases that Term, among them the first few of the post-September 11 cases challenging the constitutionality of the detention of suspected terrorists, and a father's challenge to the constitutionality of the recitation in public schools of the Pledge of Allegiance with its phrase "under God." I will probably not see another year in which the daily level of urgency and importance of the work seems as unrelenting.

Walking up those blinding white steps each day, I felt the weight of this once in a lifetime experience. I relished every moment in Justice Souter's chambers. The restrained elegance of his legal mind combined with his noble compassion and high literary style bred in those around him an aspiration to both humility and greatness, a sense of duty and sacrifice to institutions and traditions that can make people and society great. Many times when I ask myself as a check how Justice Souter would think and behave, the embodied integrity and grace of his example is a beacon for night navigation.

When my clerkship at the Supreme Court ended, I felt strongly that I wanted to know a different part of the legal system. I wanted to experience directly the everyday rough and tumble world of local criminal law enforcement, which was far from the abstractions of legal study at Harvard and the rarified air of the highest federal courts on which I had worked. At the Supreme Court, law was essentially ideas and the written

Law Clerks, Supreme Court of the United States, Washington D. C. 2004.

word, with sharp focus on sophisticated and highly cultivated reasoning in legal briefs and opinions. I loved that. But my hunger now was to experience a different aspect of the exercise of state power.

Why did I gravitate toward criminal law and criminal court? Actually I believe my obsession with the nature of language and how words and interpretation produce meaning drove this. I began with literal acquisition of a new language, moved to the study of literary language, and eventually to the language of the law. The legal theorist Robert Cover drew our attention to a basic and stark difference between literary and legal language. He wrote, famously: "Legal interpretation takes place in a field of pain and death……Legal interpretive acts signal and occasion the imposition of violence upon others. A judge articulates his understanding of a text, and as a result, somebody loses his freedom, his property, his children, even his life."

This character of legal language is why I am a lawyer. Law is "performative," in philosopher J. L. Austin's sense, in that the words do not just describe things but actually do things. And to do those things requires the threat of state imposed violence even when it is not used. I wanted to do the quotidian work of law enforcement, to understand through experience what it means for a person to wield state power, not only through written legal decrees, but as a live personification of the violence of the state.

In my first day in criminal court doing arraignments as a new prosecutor in the Manhattan District Attorney's Office, I experienced just that. A man I was arraigning for drug possession really did not want to go to jail. I asked the judge to set bail, and the judge did so. It was obvious that the man would not be able to afford the amount of bail set. It was time for him be taken to jail. He lunged toward me, knocking down my podium.

Before I knew it, six police officers appeared and mightily struggled with this man, their batons and guns drawn, pepper spray went all over the courtroom, and there was general panic and pandemonium. What made an impression on me was how long and how much force it took for six police officers to subdue and handcuff one man determined to physically resist the loss of his liberty. After this struggle ended, everyone resumed their places in the courtroom and continued the orderly process from where it was interrupted. Bail was reset in an even higher amount, given what the defendant had just done in the courtroom, and he was taken to jail like the others.

With Justice David Souter, Supreme Court of the United States.

As a rookie prosecutor with hundreds of misdemeanors to prosecute, I had the sense of literally having moved from the highest court in the land to the lowest. In the luxurious, abstract work at the Supreme Court, every argument in every case was burnished like a rare gem. In local criminal court, it was a press of the seat of your pants, messy, rough, and imperfect encounters with actual people who inhabit the criminal justice system—police, defendants, victims, witnesses, attorneys, bailiffs, bondsmen, court reporters, and trial judges. Rookies like me prosecuted domestic violence crimes, street crimes, drug crimes, and vice crimes. We read defendants their *Miranda* rights and interrogated them, interviewed police, tracked down victims for their testimony, and made plea bargains.

The defendants I prosecuted were accused of theft, prostitution, street violence, drug possession and dealing, fraud, making and selling counterfeit goods, harassment, child abuse, and domestic violence. These crimes and their consequences were not mere words. Arrests, prosecutions, convictions, and punishment had effects on real human beings, as did the crimes of which defendants were accused. People accused of stealing cans of soup, having sex for money, and hitting their children were criminal defendants and they were also human beings who wept, and whose families wept, as the routine weight of criminal justice descended on them.

The domestic violence prosecutions I conducted and observed provided a most vivid window into a distinctive developing legal regime that exercises state power in service of a well wrought social theory: legal feminism, which has had revolutionary influence on the law since the 1970s. I wanted to understand the consequences of this social movement on law and legal culture—both intended and unintended. I observed that in the quotidian enforcement of domestic violence, criminal law was shifting from its traditional goal of punishing violent conduct, in favor of exerting state control over private rights and relationships in the home. Out of this experience came the idea to write an article exploring the implications of increasing state control of the home through the law of domestic violence.

I visited my teacher Bill Stuntz up at Harvard to share with him my worries about the article I was thinking about writing. I thought it might be controversial and might rub some women's advocates fighting against domestic violence the wrong way. He looked at me and told me not to be afraid—that I was lucky to have an instinct for unexpected and surprising observations, and that it was important to develop rather than suppress it.

Applying for a Faculty Position

As I made progress on my writing, I made plans to apply for law teaching jobs in the fall of 2005. I was pregnant though, and my pregnancy was not uncomplicated. I felt sick almost all the time. I couldn't stand or walk on the street without feeling I would keel over. I had some pregnancy-related health issues, not at all life-threatening, but stressful, uncomfortable, and challenging. I had previously had one early miscarriage. It had not been devastating but it made me worry. I left my job after a short time as prosecutor to stay home and take care of my health for the months leading up to the birth.

I worked every day at my desk at home, and as my belly grew, I began to produce the article that would be the basis of an eventual job talk—the presentation at law schools to which I would apply for teaching positions, in which the candidate presents her work to the faculty and answers the faculty's questions about it. The job talk paper is one of the most important snapshots of an academic career, and functions as the essential calling card of the candidate. By the time I could feel the baby moving and kicking, the paper was under way. To be able to apply for academic jobs in the fall, I would need to complete the paper before my baby was born in late summer.

A couple weeks before the baby's due date, I was days away from finishing the job talk paper. While I was typing, my laptop made a subtle clicking noise and then went completely dark. It would not turn back on! I had been careless and not backed up the paper in another place. Had six months of work disappeared? My efforts to retrieve the data with the help of computer professionals was unsuccessful. They said they could retrieve nothing. There was nothing to be done. My paper was gone. Disappeared, just like that. I would not be able to apply for jobs as I had planned. It was a disaster! And I alone was completely to blame for neglecting to back up the files on my computer.

My son Jaemin was born after forty-two hours of very difficult labor. When he appeared he looked right into my eyes and blinked twice. I fell head over heels for him. His name is comprised of the two characters *issul jae* and *hanul min*. I explain the name's meaning to those who ask as "existence in the heavens." It is a Korean name that is beautiful as well in English, and in Hebrew as "Yamin," which means right hand. In the Jewish naming tradition, he was also named after his paternal great grandfather James, and his paternal great great grandfather David who provided Jaemin's middle name.

I was physically and mentally exhausted by the birth. I felt as though I had run a marathon and then been hit by a truck. I could barely stand up and had trouble not bursting into tears at any small decision that had to be made. My mother came to help with the baby. She had so many ideas about what should and should not be done. She insisted that I eat seaweed soup at every meal until I just couldn't take it anymore.

I wanted to breastfeed my baby and she was firmly convinced that was not possible and shouldn't even be attempted. She had not done it in Seoul in the 1970s and she claimed that our family's women were just incapable of producing milk. We struggled over this. But I went ahead and breastfed my baby for seven months. What took me by surprise was that it was among the most beautiful experiences of my life. I wish I could bottle the sensory remembrance of nursing my baby in silent intimacy, both of us half-dreaming and holding on in the dark early morning hours. It induces goose bumps to remember such tenderness.

In the fall, my former teachers at Harvard began to inquire about the state of my job talk paper. Could they read it, they asked. I was too embarrassed to tell them the truth—that I had written the paper but the computer crashed, I had not backed up, and thus had no paper and could not apply for jobs. It would be like saying the dog ate my homework. I felt like such a dolt. The best laid plans······I took a deep breath. I did not tell them. Instead, I said I just had a baby and would not be ready to apply for a teaching position for some time.

At home with my baby, my mother, and a nanny, I set to work at my desk again, trying to recreate the paper I lost. After ninety minutes of work, it would be time to feed the baby, and I would need to break for an hour to do so. I repeated this all day long for four months, and then the paper was finally finished again. It was probably better for having been done twice.

I submitted the paper to the Yale Law Journal, which agreed

to publish it. I was ready to present it. I went up to Cambridge. I could not believe I was a candidate to join my teachers on the faculty at Harvard Law School. But I was also less terrified than I had been for any performance on stage. I think my store of stage fright was depleted by those early terrors at the piano. During the breaks in the day of interviews, I had to run back to my room at the Charles Hotel in Harvard Square to pump breastmilk to store in the refrigerator for my baby. Perhaps there was just too much else to keep focus on just to get the job done, and very little space for doubt or fear.

I was in Argentina on a family vacation, pushing the stroller on the streets of Buenos Aires in front of the Casa Rosada when Elena Kagan, then Dean of Harvard Law School, called my mobile phone and told me the faculty had voted to appoint me. I joined the faculty as an Assistant Professor in July 2006.

Seven months later and eighteen months after my son, my daughter Mina was born. She was so delicious and her beauty irresistible. She too has a Korean name that works gracefully in English as well as in Yiddish. She was named after her paternal great grandmother, whose Yiddish middle name Shayna means beautiful. Mina's middle name, Zipporah, which means bird, is also from the same great grandmother, whose first name, Feigel, means bird in Yiddish. It is really a huge challenge for me not to brag about her!

There is nothing like becoming a mother to make you understand how intensely your parents have loved you. Having children and wanting to be with them sharpened the edges of the boundaries of time that I had to focus on my work. Work now needed to be concentrated and could not simply be allowed to grow like an unwieldy parasitic plant to take over every psychic corner of my world. Work had to become more of a hardy self-sustaining flower if it was going to take root and blossom. It would have to share soil and not overtake the most spectacular blooms in the garden. I know that loving my children like crazy enabled me also to understand how vital work was to me. My desire for my work was so strong that having my children made my work better and even more rewarding—because I had to learn to rule it and not let it rule me. I had to grow up.

04

Harvard

"To have doubted one's own first principles is the mark of a civilized man."
— Oliver Wendell Holmes, Jr.

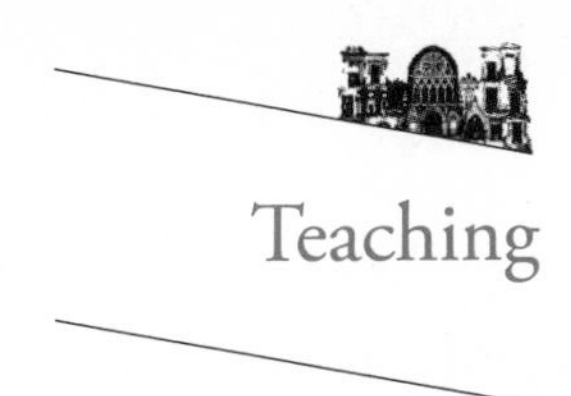

Teaching

At Harvard, I began to teach criminal law and family law. Being the teacher now in the same classrooms where I had been a student just a few years before felt both strange and natural. Many who came on the faculty before me experienced exactly this transition. I felt that being a law professor there was both a highly surprising turn of events and just what I was meant to do. Above all, my excitement at the scene of the law school classroom made me happy to wake up each morning.

I began the first day of my criminal law course with a case that involves a man committing the misdemeanor of illegal fishing. When the state officer attempts to arrest him for that crime, he resists, hits the officer with an oar, and tries to get away. The officer then shoots him in the arm. The legal question is whether the state officer was allowed to use deadly force to make an arrest of a person who committed merely a misdemeanor. The court says that to allow an individual who resists arrest to get away would be "to elevate mere brute force to a position of command over the wheels of justice." That is, to allow individual strength to resist the rule of law.

I used the case to start the criminal law course with the most basic but profound recognition that law is always potentially violent because law cannot be enforced without the state's threat of violence. Anyone who has been involved in or seen an arrest where an individual resists, passively or actively, will uncomfortably have to admit that the line between proper police protocol and police abuse does not look as obvious as we would wish it to be. Law enforcement depends on force, the ability of government to coerce individuals to obey the law and to punish if they do not. The brute fact is that individuals comply because they fear harm, and where they resist, they can be hurt. As a prosecutor in Manhattan I had been struck by the fact that arraignments of criminal defendants often take place by hospital beds, with judge, prosecutor, defense attorney, and court reporter all assembled there to arraign an individual who had been injured while resisting arrest.

The law depends on the state's ability to subdue the force of individuals. The reason the line between police brutality and justified law enforcement sometimes appears a difficult one is that law enforcement is the violence of the state. The key is to exercise this force with self-discipline and self-control, which is inherently challenging but is demanded of government every day in the enforcement of law, which after all is the imposition of constraint on every citizen in a democracy. The connection of law, violence, and governance is a lesson every student who will wield legal power needs to understand.

My former teacher Bill, now my colleague, made frequent visits to my office to offer frank advice on teaching and writing. He let me know I was taken care of and watched over by those invested in my success. I felt as if I were bathed in a warm but vigorous bath.

As a young novice teacher, it was extremely tempting to feel that I had to be, well, perfect—to know everything and to be erudite, authoritative, dignified, and polished. To be a figure Harvard Law School students could respect and admire. Well, fortunately, I was pretty soon disabused of whatever illusion of perfection there may have been. One day during my first year of teaching, I was rushing to class because I feared being

At Harvard Law School.

late, which I cannot stand. I was balancing in my hands a large casebook, an unwieldy cardboard seating chart, and a hot drink. The students were already in their seats in the amphitheater-style classroom, and hushed as I entered through the door at the back. I made my way down the stairs bisecting the length of the room toward the podium in front. Halfway down, I felt my ankle wobble a bit on a step and then fold. Suddenly, *BOOM*, I was flat on the ground, book, chart, and hot liquid flying. The students collectively gasped as I landed.

I remember thinking, "OK, I'm finished here. Can't possibly be a professor. Might as well just leave." I got up, brushed off, and went to the podium. I taught the best class I had ever taught up to that point. The course in the remainder of the semester was much more relaxed and successful than it had been previously.

I realized afterward that it had actually been a relief to fall flat on my face. It became blatantly obvious and undeniable in one fell swoop that there was no perfection here. My spectacular fall had been a literalization of the common English figure of speech, "to fall flat on one's face," which means to fail. Indeed, given the amount of energy and time that successful people spend maintaining control, composure, and aplomb, it was very telling that having the worst happen—falling flat on my face—was not the end of the world but rather a release. I believe it was a huge boon to my comfort as a teacher going forward. Everyone felt more comfortable. Everyone was human.

I associate that fall with the epiphany of my first year as a law professor: Trying to be perfect hurts. It hurts like hell. And it doesn't work. It is constraining, like wearing a corset or a hair shirt. It survives on fear. The release from myself that I experienced as a classroom teacher from having had that fall was like a deliverance. I became a good teacher, more genuinely able to connect with my students in the classroom. The girl who spent childhood often speechless and alienated in the classroom somehow became able to work happily in a job that demanded verbal mastery and powers of communication in the classroom. The free air I could now breathe comfortably there, I wanted to breathe elsewhere too.

My writing too began to take off. The writerly demons slunk away. In my office at Harvard, I did not feel blocked anymore. I began to feel joy writing in my quiet space. I had back that compelling pleasure that I had as a child library reader and a teenage ballet student. The discipline of working with focus to learn and create through research and writing was intensely pleasurable. When the day began, I looked forward to the hours I would spend at my desk working in detail through texts and ideas. It was just so much fun. Writing will never come easily or fast for me, but I can now say it is one of the most enjoyable activities I know.

I walked around Harvard campus with a huge smile on my face, incredulous that I was so lucky to have landed in a place in the world that gave me such space and freedom to do work I loved to do—work I would most want to do under any circumstances. And I felt blessedly free to follow my fascinations where they led.

During my first semester of teaching, the actor Alec Baldwin paid me a visit in my office at Harvard to speak with me about the book he was writing, *A Promise to Ourselves*, about his divorce and legal struggles over custody of his daughter. We discoursed for hours about the relation between feminist legal reform, criminal law, family law, and the legal treatment of fathers and mothers in child custody disputes. I invited Alec to come speak to my class about his experiences in the family law system and his work as an advocate of shared parenting. We led together a Socratic dialogue, questioning and probing each other and the students about these ideas. The resulting classroom discussion was electric. In the startlingly broad-ranging conversations between us that ensued, he had the idea to represent in the book in some way the dialogue in which we were engaged.

A chapter of Alec's book, called "A Trip to Cambridge," tells the story of his coming to speak to my students at Harvard, and then features a conversation and a series of questions and answers between Alec and me. In his book telling his own story, Alec attempted to connect with ordinary readers about the phenomenon of divorce, but also to explore its universality and explore some problems in the legal system through the telling of his experience in it. He wanted to express empathy and support for fathers who truly wanted to parent their children meaningfully after divorce. I respected his doing this. Working with Alec helped me see that many of the legal issues in criminal law and family law in which I was becoming expert were not only the stuff of legal theory, but also issues of everyday life that cut to the core of what many people care most about, the problems and dilemmas that get them where they live.

The project I had developed in my job talk paper became the core of my book, *At Home in the Law*, which was an exploration of the legal meaning of home in a range of contemporary problems connected to criminal law. What was the home, I asked. At least as early as the sixteenth century, we had in the Anglo-American tradition, the adage that a man's house is his castle. This meant that the house was a fortress against invasion from other people, but equally important, it was a bulwark against even the king. This concept had legal consequences for what was considered criminal, and it made invasion of the castle in warfare a model of what crime is. It also made clear that freedom from the reach of government depended on this boundary.

The home was also the nineteenth-century bourgeois ideal of domesticity and privacy, the affective space of the family, closely associated with women, the human embodiment of domesticity. The home marked the literal and metaphorical boundary of what was considered private and what was considered public. The home as the quintessentially private space has been central to key concepts in many areas of law—crime, sex, liberty, and property.

The home as a concept had a paradox embedded in it. It was supposed to be the place of ultimate security, comfort, and familiarity. But it could also be the opposite, fraught with feelings of terror and vulnerability. This was the creepy feeling that Freud called the *unheimlich*: the creepy feeling when the thing that is most familiar and home-like becomes also the opposite, so that home is transformed into not-home. It was both safe and frightening, familiar and strange at the same time.

I found this concept of the *unheimlich*, or in English the uncanny, helpful for understanding a move that feminist critique performed on the home concept to reimagine the home, the domestic space of affective privacy, as a kind of prison for women and the place of their subordination. Since the 1970s in the U. S., feminism sought to make interventions in legal institutions and succeeded in some crucial places. And this success has focused in large part on the home.

One consequence of this transformation is that along with the home, the closely associated concept of privacy came under attack. It was because of the conceptual distinction between the private and the public that runs through our legal system that the criminal justice system did not intervene when women were being beaten by their husbands. Legal feminists therefore criticized the idea of home privacy, and wanted the state to see a woman being beaten in the home as just as much a matter of public interest as violence on the public street.

At Home in the Law argued that the idea of home most powerfully shaping law and legal discourse today is that of violence within domestic space. Home as violence—indeed an uncanny transformation. This growing legal vision, which has justified increasing state control of the home, has led to substantial reduction of autonomy and privacy of both women and men in relation to the state, especially in immigrant and minority communities already subject to disproportionate state control and police observation.

At Home in the Law was finished seven years after Bill saw a draft of the little student paper that first began my thinking on law and the home. But I had been working on the concept of home and its representation during my studies in literature for years before that. The homeland of my infancy, the new home of the immigrant, home and colonialism, fleeing home, home and exile, home nostalgia, home as country, home as family, home as privacy. Of course. The thread was obvious and easy to trace once revealed. Without planning or knowing it, I had been bridging several different continents, disciplines, and languages following this thread. It was unmistakable.

I realized that my project as a law professor was to speak in multiple disciplinary languages. The law regulates our lives by

"I hope for young people to have opportunities to discover and pursue what they love—the ideas, activities, passions, and thoughts that make them fully human."

© Michael Malyszko 2007

giving effect to cultural values and concepts that students of the humanities, novelists, and poets also interrogate. What does it mean to be human? How does human beings' production of meaning affect how we govern ourselves? I have written about not only what the law is, but also how legal actors understand and describe the ideas and concepts that justify the law and make it intelligible.

One of my articles, *The Trajectory of Trauma: Bodies and Minds of Abortion Discourse*, was about the legal discourse of abortion—that is, the language and ideas that legal actors use to describe the meaning of abortion in the course of making arguments about the constitutionality of legal restrictions on abortion. I analyzed how legal actors describe the harm caused by abortion. Increasingly, rather than emphasizing the killing of the fetus, advocates, lawmakers, and judges in the U. S., including the Supreme Court emphasize psychological trauma to the woman who has an abortion, as a way of understanding why it might be rational for legislatures to pass laws limiting abortion—to protect women from psychological harm. I showed that the rise of this legal discourse of trauma that is now being used to restrict the right to abortion, reflects the influence of legal feminist discourse we have seen in domestic violence, sexual harassment, and rape law reform, presenting women as exemplary sufferers of psychological trauma in matters having to do with violation of the body. I believe that lawyers need to be able to see the relations between our technical modes of reasoning and the broader ideas that motivate us and shape what it means to be human. I try in my work to forge and explicate those connections.

This effort to study the law in an interdisciplinary frame has also informed my work on intellectual property in an article, *The Law, Culture, and Economics of Fashion*. Fashion is one of the world's most creative industries. The global apparel, shoes, accessories business has U. S. sales larger than those of books, movies, and music combined. Everyone's apparel involves both cultural norms and individual choice. Thus fashion is a phenomenon that is nearly universal. My coauthor Scott Hemphill, a professor at Columbia Law School, was a close friend from the time when we were law clerks together on the Supreme Court—he for Justice Scalia and I for Justice Souter. Our chambers were adjacent to each other that year. Since then we had wanted to work on something together and this was the project we chose.

We began by asking, what is fashion? On one hand, it's a most immediate way in which people express who they are as individuals. But on the other hand, it's a way in which people also strive to be in conformity with other people. In fashion, people flock together to the new, then that fascination subsides, and they move onto something else. Fashion is a version of a ubiquitous phenomenon, the ebb and flow of trends wherein the new becomes old and then leads to the new. In that way, fashion provides a window into culture and creativity, the way humans behave and make meaning in social life.

Like all of the creative arts, fashion design involves borrowing and influence from existing works and themes in the culture. But Scott and I wanted to understand why intellectual property law deems its effects on the incentives of original creators of fashion design to be different from those of original creators of books, music, movies, architecture, and choreography. Our article participated in ongoing policy debates on copyright protection for fashion design. I had the chance to testify in Congress about our proposal of a narrow new copyright for fashion design, tailored to reflect the ways in which fashion is like and unlike the dynamics of copying in other creative arts industries.

My interest in the arts has informed my teaching, and Harvard has been very open to the creation of new courses in the curriculum, such as my course on Performing Arts and Law. I co-taught this course with Damian Woetzel, the ballet star whom I had watched, agog, countless times on the stage of the New York State Theater in my twenties. As teenagers we each attended SAB. He went on to become a principal dancer of the New York City Ballet. I still remember particular performances that stopped me in my tracks. He was an artist of god-like dimensions.

During my second year as a professor, I met Damian at a party at Harvard, where he studied for a master's degree in public policy after retiring from the stage in his late 30s. We decided to team up to teach the first Performing Arts course at Harvard Law School. The course explored several aspects of performance: philosophical questions of what "performance" is, and what it means to perform; legal topics in the law of performance, focusing on intellectual property and labor; and finally ways in which scenes of performance and ritual constitute lawyerly activity and legal processes such as trial. So many of our students had pursued a passion for art making—in music, dance, film, and theater—prior to entering the law. It was amazing fun to be able to channel our arts obsessions into the pedagogy of the law school classroom.

"Above all, my excitement at the scene of the law school classroom made me happy to wake up each morning."

© Michael Malyszko 2007

Damian began our first class by teaching our students to dance the sublime opening measures of *Serenade*, right hands and eyes raised to the sky. We invited distinguished guests to speak to the class, including the Lincoln Center General Counsel Leslie Rosenthal, former Metropolitan Opera head Joseph Volpe, playwright John Guare, jazz saxophonist Joshua Redman, and actor Alec Baldwin. Doing this project with Damian, one of the foremost living artistic interpreters of Balanchine, and our wonderful students at Harvard Law School, I couldn't believe how lucky I was.

Harvard Law School

In the fall of 2010, on the basis of my scholarly output in four years as an Assistant Professor, my senior colleagues voted tenure for me, and I was promoted to a tenured position as Professor of Law.

Some friends who have attained tenure report that it did not make much of a difference in how they felt in their jobs and in their life. For me, though, it has been a source of unabashed excitement and happiness. I enjoy and appreciate it each day. Though I already felt I had great freedom to think, speak, and write on whatever I wished, tenure lifted any remnants of hesitation. It strongly affirmed that what I wanted for my life was exactly what tenure is supposed to bestow: a freedom meant to push the work that lies ahead to be better and more innovative than what came before. It was the ultimate gift that a person who wants to live a life of the mind can receive. I marvel at the form of life it enables.

I was now truly colleagues with my teachers and mentors. From Morty and Lani to Janet and Bill, and many others I have not mentioned, teachers saw me through, raised me, and showed me to think and do things I didn't imagine before. They helped me grow up from an insecure student to become their peer. I was surrounded by beneficence and warmth. Care for my intellectual development and my voice, as well as for my growth as an adult. A sense of being entrusted with the future. This is the profound feeling I hope to create as a teacher to my students.

Bill's cancer diagnosis, after years of his unending back pain, was agony for me and for our colleagues. The suffering of Job came to our minds. But Bill managed to teach and write brilliantly through it all, as his body shrunk with the treatment and multiple complicated surgeries. His students adored him to distraction. His walks through the halls to visit colleagues to discuss their work never stopped. If I asked how he was feeling, he just wanted to talk about teaching, writing, and the school.

When the faculty voted tenure for me, Bill knew he wouldn't be here long. He warned me that I had developed a distinctive scholarly voice and was good at what I had done so far, but to live up to my potential, I had to be more ambitious in my subjects and methods in the future. He was right of course, but he wouldn't be here to see this happen.

My office at Harvard Law School is in Griswold Hall, which was named for Dean Erwin Griswold, who led the school from the 1940s to the 1960s. It was during this period under his deanship that women students were first admitted to the school. He oversaw the breaking of this gender barrier in 1950 and felt responsibility for it. A famous story about Dean Griswold that is legendary and apparently true is that that each year he invited the then-small handful of women students in the Harvard Law School class to his house for dinner, and then sitting with them in a circle in his living room, asked each to justify taking the place of a man.

The story, recounted by many rounds of women who were students at Harvard Law School in the 1950s and 1960s, is startling to our modern ears. His question sounds hostile and assumes that women's place is not naturally or properly in a law school. But the question also presupposes that when

At Harvard Study. 2010.[10]

this education and opportunity is offered to you, you have a responsibility to use it to contribute greatly to society(rather than staying home and raising children, to state the relevant alternative). I find the story an ambivalent one that expresses both the threatened anxiety about women entering traditionally male educational and professional worlds, and also the urging of elite women to take their places boldly in public life as elite men traditionally had the duty to do.

My mentor Lani Guinier became the first African American woman tenured at Harvard Law School shortly before I was a student there. I was given my first academic job by the first female Dean of Harvard Law School, Elena Kagan, now Justice Kagan on the Supreme Court of the United States. During this time, the country elected the first African American President of the United States, a graduate of Harvard Law School and the first African American president of the Harvard Law Review. I was tenured under the first female President of Harvard University, Drew Faust, and the second female Dean of Harvard Law School, Martha Minow. I am the first East Asian tenured faculty member, the first Asian woman, and the first Korean on the law school faculty.

When I was granted tenure, my appointment became

news in Korea. I was caught by surprise. I was asked so many questions by Koreans who wanted to know about how I got here, what it meant to me, what my childhood was like, and what my parents were like. Most professors do not encounter this kind of interest. But Koreans and Harvard, it seemed, were an irresistible pairing. Koreans revered Harvard like almost no other institution in the world because of what it represented to them—excellence in education and scholarship. This reverence was a fact deeply ingrained in modern Korean values and mythology, connected to its particular feudal past, in which study and scholarly attainment were so highly valued that they placed a family in the highest echelons of the social order. It forced me to reflect on the questions that were now being asked of me—what it meant to come from a community that produced me and had a claim on me, and to represent a group's gratification and pride.

I realized that being a Korean, a minority, and a woman were not things I thought about on a daily basis as I went about my business doing the work I needed and wanted to do. And I knew that was yet another of the many ways in which I benefited from the freedom of being born and raised in times and places where it was not a huge novelty or exclusionary barrier to be who I was in the educational contexts I was lucky

In Seoul, 2011.[11]

Speaking to the Korean Harvard Law School Alumni Association, Seoul, 2011. [12]

enough to inhabit. Yet it was so obvious the ways in which the particular history, values, and traditions of Korean society and culture—some of them well-known and stereotypical—were the fabric of my childhood and still provided rich figures with which I jousted and grappled all the time.

The initial jolt of being thus interpellated settled into a calmer self-recognition. I was not just myself making my own merry way through life. The immense freedom I enjoyed in my thoughts, work, and play was the product of people, cultures, values, practices, and contingencies that were owed some reflection. Anything outstanding or typical about me was completely embedded inside those facts when I looked closely.

Indeed I was a minority, an immigrant, and a woman in a traditionally male and white bastion of elite privilege, an institution that is in many ways changed but in many ways unchanged. What accounted for my feelings of belonging and comfort there? Why didn't I have the experience of exclusion? Instead why did I thrive? I know that much of the explanation lies in the human fact of my being embraced by my teachers first as their student, and then as part of a long line of teachers extending backward and forward, within a noble project to produce knowledge and to educate. And in turn I embraced back. But I also know that for generations women and minorities have not felt fully welcome or at home in this institution.

Perhaps for this reason, when Dean Kagan began her deanship, one visible change in the law school was the replacement of some of the old gilded paintings of famous dead white men of the law that hung in the school's public spaces, with art that was apparently intended to project a more "modern" or "neutral" image of the school. The old paintings went into storage in a basement of the library, and the collection was then rumored to be on the verge of acquisition by Sotheby's or Christie's. One of these now-demoted paintings was a life-size portrait of the seventeenth-century Lord Chief Justice of England, Sir Matthew Hale, decked out in scarlet judicial regalia and fur mantle. I remembered the portrait of the jurist hanging prominently in Langdell Library when I was a student.

I took over my office in Griswold from retired Professor Charles Haar with whom I had worked as a student editor of the Harvard Law Review when we published one of his final scholarly articles. The office had been his since the building opened in 1979, the year I came to the U. S. as a six-year-old child. A wall of the office was large and blank when I moved

The Korea Economic Institute(KEI) has honored Korean Americans from government, business, academia, arts and literature. [13]

in. I thought of the large painting and wondered where it was languishing, banished from a place of honor. The library allowed me to borrow the portrait to hang in my office. It is very impressive on my wall and looks like it belongs right there. Lord Hale and I exchange meaningful glances as I write at my desk. I wrote my dissertation in the libraries of Oxford where he studied. I am the one who is here now at Harvard Law School. His legacy is in part at the mercy of the likes of me.

Hale's famous treatise, *The History of the Pleas of the Crown*, is a text to which many criminal law teachers refer—certainly I do in several parts of the criminal law course, in pointing students to legal forerunners in the form of traditional English common law formulations. The particular reason I can think of for relegating Hale to the basement is that one of his many statements has become notorious in the past generation as a reflection of a traditional antiquated attitude toward women that now appears hopelessly sexist—like many gendered assumptions undergirding the common law: that rape "is an accusation easily to be made and hard to be proved, and harder to be defended by the party accused, tho never so innocent."

I teach rape law in my criminal law class, of course. That it is easy to accuse someone of rape may not be true, but examination of the ways in which an accusation may be hard to prove and hard to defend against, and of how changing social understandings of sex and gender affect legal rules, are precisely the stuff of a good law school class. I surmise that some students have wondered with feminist dismay that I would have a portrait of Matthew Hale in my office. The reason to have such a portrait in the space where I work is not to celebrate or lionize, but rather to recognize that our project is the understanding and critique of an evolving tradition with which we struggle and argue.

Roscoe Pound, a past Dean of Harvard Law School, said, "The law must be stable but it must not stand still." When I teach students in the classroom, I am keenly aware that we work together in a living tradition that has produced and will produce generations of leaders and innovators to whom they are connected, those who safeguard the law's stability but also push it not to stand still. People who evolve the way we think, change our world, and secure its future. Law teachers teach critical engagement with our legal tradition. The portrait stands for this, like the ambivalence of Dean Griswold's question to women students, similarly antiquated yet still resonant and unresolved.

I have a fortunate life, blessed with what Koreans untranslatably call *oon*. Not many bad things had happened to me. But in the time and space of finding a truly good place as a teacher, scholar, and mother in so many ways—having two young children, growing into my profession, learning to write more easily, and achieving tenure—with everything happening all at once, my marriage—and great love—unraveled. The wrenching experience of losing a marriage will be a sadness of my life, which I accept, as I do the joy and meaning I undeniably have. We will indeed grow old as parents to our children and good friends always, but not together in the ways we imagined. Any appearance that one is charmed or perfect must fall away, and then one sees that real life, with its visible and indelible imperfections, has been there all along.

My teacher Bill Stuntz died in 2011. I got the phone call in Paris during spring break, and before the words were even said tears fell on my dress. That semester at Harvard, I was in the midst of teaching the criminal adjudication course that Bill was regularly scheduled to teach. Bill had come to my office, all skin and bones from his chemotherapy, to ask me to take over the course in his place. He apologized that his illness was so advanced that he would likely not be alive to teach the course. A week before I began teaching for Bill, I found on the chair in my office some yellow pads of paper containing his own

Dad's 60th Birthday, New York 2007.

handwritten teaching notes. Bill had left the treasures for me with a little post-it that said: "I doubt these will be useful but just in case."

I didn't see him after that. He had gone home one winter evening after his last walk of the halls. I was asked for a sentence or two to be quoted in Harvard Law School's announcement of Bill's passing from colon cancer at age 52. In a daze I said some things in my role as his former student and mentee. But the words came out as lifeless formulas in eulogy.

Bill's posthumously published book, *The Collapse of American Criminal Justice* represents the scholarly majesty of Bill, who inspired many students' study and work in criminal justice. Bill decried the U. S. legal system's overreliance on criminal law, calling criminal punishment "a necessary but terrible thing—to be used sparingly, not promiscuously."

Bill was drawn to notice pathologies and paradoxes in how criminal law is made and enforced. One characteristic insight was that the U. S. Supreme Court's liberal expansion of constitutional rights protections for criminal defendants in the 1960s, motivated by concern to protect racial minorities and poor people from unfair treatment by government, led legislatures to increase criminal sentences and expand crimes' definitions so more people would be arrested and imprisoned longer. Thus the protection of criminal defendants' rights resulted in more arrests and harsher punishment of minorities and poor people. Bill taught my generation to pay attention to how the unexpected consequences of an action can be the opposite of the intent because of perverse political and economic incentives.

When a teacher dies, the student experiences a distinctive loss—the loss of time in which the student might have repaid, to even the score of generosity. With Bill this loss is all the more painful because his giving expanded through years of suffering in which he never stopped offering up his inspiring intellectual bounty and moral decency, while the rest of us struggled just to manage our schedules.

At Harvard Law School it is traditional for students to applaud the teacher at the end of the last class of the semester. Bill's teaching notes included a speech for the final class in which he told students that he did not want applause because learning was not like being a spectator at a performance. Rather it was a shared mutual conversation in which students taught him as much as he taught them. I know the students didn't believe they taught their professor, but I also know he believed with sincere gratitude that he learned hugely from them.

My next book will have to come into existence after Bill's death, yet I hope it will be a step toward the ambition he urged me to have. It is a book that tells the story of the growing influence of the concept of post-traumatic stress in the legal system. Colloquially, trauma may refer to an emotionally distressing or shocking experience. Psychiatrists first used the designation post-traumatic stress disorder(PTSD) to diagnose troubled Vietnam War veterans, and to describe when memory of an event causes suffering from uncontrollable symptoms such as depression, anxiety, nightmares, flashbacks, and insomnia. Although the psychological problems of veterans drove the push for the professional recognition of the PTSD diagnosis, it has been the women's movement—with its focus on sexual violence—that has carried the language of trauma into both popular and legal conceptions of harm. Sex for women and war for men are the twin paths along which the idea of trauma has developed.

Trauma has unprecedented currency in our time. A concept that our parents' generation barely knew has become ubiquitous in public discourse and in our law. Beyond the

Speech at The Woman of TIME Award. [14]

extremities of rape and war, trauma has increasingly become a common language in which our legal system and our culture make sense of how experiencing or witnessing events can harm people emotionally and later cause them to harm others. My next book will tell the story of how trauma came to have this pull over us, to become our default manner of framing events that challenge or overwhelm us, in both ordinary and extraordinary life experience? The massive social and legal influence of trauma, essentially a theory of memory and its psychic effects, is transforming our basic sense of what it means to be harmed and what it means to be responsible—ideas that constitute law and society's views of the human.

Oliver Wendell Holmes, Jr. wrote that a person "may live greatly in the law as well as elsewhere." For me the study of legal ideas and the teaching of law students are ways of aspiring to live greatly in the law.

But first, a school. I believe in that. It is a school that forms the people who will give life to the institutions that secure tradition and make change: the minds and the bodies, the values and the aesthetics, the technical skills and the innovative leaps, the intellectual habits and the social customs. A school is the foundation for society, its practices, norms, and aspirations.

First and Foremost a Teacher

First and foremost, I am a teacher at a school. That is my most important professional role. In the classroom, I try to teach students to understand the awesome responsibility and power they will have, as some of the most influential legal actors in the world. Serving as a guide for young minds as they experience afresh the joy and fascination of thinking will never grow tired. To do this work now in the school that gave me so much, that formed my legal mind, the place where American legal education was invented, is the privilege of my life. What this privilege means to me is to reflect through teaching and writing on the legal traditions through which we govern ourselves, and the rule of law in our world.

What is a legal education for? It is not just a fancy credential or pedigree. It is a profound intellectual and socializing process. I think law school is one of the most transformative and thrilling educational processes known to man. If law professors teach anything important, it's not information students can just as well learn from books. What we teach is a method of thinking, a habit of reasoning that can lead one to doubt one's own first principles.

The students do not cut apart a physical cadaver as do their counterparts in medical school. But they learn to dissect the structures of power, authority, legitimacy and meaning that underlie our society. This is what makes the job of the lawyer so fundamental in a democratic society. To learn it, you can't just study it in books, you have to experience it, as live performance where students are not spectators but active participants. That's what makes it fun.

Our practical reason begins in the classroom, in live engagement, interaction, disagreement, discussion, and reconsideration. The case method of study was invented by Harvard Law School Dean Christopher Columbus Langdell in the late nineteenth century and perfected in a form known as the Socratic Method, which is today the standard pedagogy of U.

S. legal education. Instead of lecturing to students, the Socratic teacher explores actual cases in a live dialogue with the student, and in discussion in front of the class.

What the Socratic method has in common with Socrates's dialogues is that the teacher asks questions to which there is neither a right answer nor an ultimate one. How it differs is that the dialogue is not a pure reasoned inquiry into the abstract principles of truth. It is simultaneously more restricted, more practical, and arguably more important. It is the inquiry into what Sir Edward Coke, the seventeenth-century Lord Chief Justice of England, called the "artificial reason" of the law. Why is law "artificial reason"? It is not pure reason. Law does of course depend on logic, but it is not the reinvention of first principles. Instead it builds upon past acts and ideas: precedents, traditions, and reasoning. And this is subject to judgment of their practical consequences in the world.

Rather than simply teach what the law is, we teach how—how to think about problems that don't have clear answers. When our students graduate, their technical legal skills are unparalleled. But they are not simply preparing to be rote appliers of law. In our ever-changing world, they will be entrusted with the institutions and legal frameworks that

"Like everything else, it takes practice—willing oneself to do it again and again until it becomes much easier, even enjoyable."

At Harvard Study. 2010.

make our society possible. They will use their imagination and courage to solve new problems whose contours we don't even know yet. So they must learn to think broadly, through but also beyond technique, about institutions that effect actions.

We train lawyers to think, but unlike their counterparts in other disciplines, their reasoning can also become acts, channeled through the authority and force of government institutions, with real consequences for people's lives. Will our students become not only professionals with breathtaking technical skills, but also people of integrity who can wield the law with practical wisdom, discipline, and mercy? Will they be people we can trust?

But first, a school. A law school is at the center of a society that is governed through laws, and a constitutional culture committed to the rule of law. The training of lawyers is vitally important, and I am proud to engage in this process as my life's work. I love to look out at my students and know they are indispensable to the guardianship of institutions that make society possible. I am proud to impress on them a responsibility to serve the world that has given them so much opportunity to develop their minds and their characters. They can do so much in so many places in the world. The students, past, present and future make real the school's aspirations. The students are the reasons for my optimism. They are my sources of inspiration.

“We all have to make choices about how to configure our lives.”

Advice to Young Korean Students

My dean, Dean Martha Minow welcomes our students to the school by telling them: "We searched the world for you." Undoubtedly one of the highest educational priorities today is to advance global engagement. In some ways, the U. S. law school classroom demands certain behavior from which many Korean students have been discouraged in their upbringing as children in a Korean family. For example, at home I was punished if I tried to debate and argue about ideas with a person to whom I was supposed to show respect. Some of my Korean students tell me that they are "just not good at" public speaking and therefore plan to pursue careers that will not require that of them. But of course there is a range among Korean students, and some of them appear to have no trouble with this in law school.

The advice I most frequently give Korean students is that they should push themselves to seek opportunities to learn to do what makes them uncomfortable—whether it is speaking in public or writing. Like everything else, it takes practice—willing oneself to do it again and again until it becomes much easier, even enjoyable. I am aggravated when students assume that their diffidence in the classroom is an issue of some personal quality or defect. It is not. It is a matter of cultural difference and upbringing. It poses real challenges that are surmountable. Students must learn to master different ways of learning and behaving by doing, much like walking into a classroom not speaking the language, and eventually speaking it as well or better than the others. You speak the language that works in the particular context, and learn the flexibility to switch as needed. It is not a matter of one way being right and the other being wrong. It is a matter of fluency—a form of cultural fluency not unlike being able to speak multiple languages. Gaining one fluency does not have to mean losing the other, though of course a person is changed and moved by the process.

Koreans are fortunate to be steeped complexly in a culture

with such a compelling combination of traditionalism and a drive to innovation. What is challenging for young people is grappling with the expectations of their parents, families, and communities, while also fanning the inner spark of creativity and imagination. I am often asked by young Koreans reaching adulthood how to reconcile their own desires for their lives and the wishes of their parents. It is common for young people to experience struggles and conflicts in the course of finding their voices. Often parents do not know best. Sometimes success and fulfillment in a path requires not adhering to behavior that was encouraged at home. Taking risks and making one's own mistakes are essential.

When I'm in the middle of work that I have chosen out of desire, I cannot wait to get to work each day. It makes me feel alive and fully human. It makes me want to do the best I can. There are so many different paths to a good life. We need to resist the tendency to think there is one right way to do things. Koreans are taking the lead in so many different fields, in an astonishing range of endeavors. We need to pursue all of those diverse ways of contributing to our global world.

When a professor is granted tenure at Harvard Law School, a photo portrait of her goes up in the hall of the school. It is a

At Harvard Study. 2010.

"Whatever the path, conflict and failure are not the end of the world."

At Harvard Study. 2010.

tradition. The portrait is for posterity, and remains hanging there even after the professor's departure, retirement, or death. Mine is among the newest up there in the long line of law teachers at Harvard. Sometimes as I pass by it on my way to teach, a group of Koreans visiting on a tour of Harvard campus are gathered there, snapping photographs of this portrait of me. I suppose that to them it is a symbol of Korean success in the United States. I understand that what is interesting is not me, exactly, but what my position represents in the educational values that are so pronounced and deeply embedded in Korean society. I am very honored by Koreans' attention, and think it speaks volumes about Korean culture that a professor who works in a university, a place for research, teaching, and the production of knowledge, can inspire such admiration. But the job I do is basically solitary—working in my office on research, teaching, and writing most of the time. That is why I am here.

My parents tell me that had we remained in Korea I would likely not have had great success in the Korean school system. My particular set of qualities and strengths, my ways of thinking, and what I consider important would not have been highly prized in the world of Korean scholastic achievement. My poor study habits as a youngster, inability to memorize things, incessant questioning, tendency to distraction and multiple pursuits, and lackluster test-taking instincts would have finished me early on.

Perhaps these stereotypes of Korean education are not accurate anymore. Perhaps it is no longer the case that what it means for a child in Korea to study well is to memorize information by rote to perform on high-stakes exams with a tunnel vision that can stifle creativity and joy in learning.

For a time I sent my children to Korean school in Boston on Saturday mornings. They were both under six at the time. They loved learning tae kwon do there. But in the academic part of the curriculum, they spent much of the time sitting at desks copying Korean letters they didn't yet understand(they didn't know how to read English yet either). The children were given exams they were told to study for—while they weren't even kindergarten age—and they somehow developed the impression(possibly a child's imagination run amok?) that if they didn't do well on the test, something bad would happen to them, like being shamed or kicked out of the school. That wasn't fun. Learning in this way didn't feel like play, and it didn't open the mind or enter the heart. When they begged me to quit, I just had to admit they weren't tough enough for Korean school, so I let them quit. It was a pity, because I think they would have liked knowing their grandparents' native tongue. I'll try again later.

Elementary schoolchildren growing up Korea even today appear to have a significantly more austere and joyless affect with respect to school than children of the same age growing up in the U. S. But of course it is very difficult to know exactly what combination of culture, education, tradition, and social norms produce this appearance of difference, and what exactly to think of it.

What I do know is that the experience of being swept away with rapture at ideas, stories, and imagination was important in my childhood, and I can't imagine such a thing happening by authoritarian command. I was lucky that my home allowed enough freedom for a child's excitement and wonder to develop, and it was not squeezed out by a stress on arid memorization and all-or-nothing test-taking that characterized at least some visible aspects of a grinding Korean educational style that I also saw growing up. I had repeated chances to be a late bloomer and to reinvent myself. My schools and teachers gave those to me. Without those chances, I would not have been admitted to the schools that formed me, let alone become a professor. I know that my story is an American story, and it is the American university that has enabled me to thrive and discover the creative work I love.

One of the most rewarding aspects of my having immigrated to the United States as a young child with my Korean family has been the opportunity to reconnect as an adult in my own right in a special way with the country where I was born—through engagement with the Korean legal community and with Koreans' appreciation of the American journey that immigrants have taken. I am touched by their recognition and wish to do the best I can to deserve it. For me it is like tenure: a vote of confidence that the future holds great promise.

I am sometimes asked by Koreans to comment publicly on Korea—what I see as its problems, challenges, and needed changes, particularly in its education system. But I left Korea when I was a child and have not lived there for any significant time since. I wasn't educated in Korea beyond kindergarten and a few months of first grade, so of course I can't speak with deep experience of Korean education. The most visible differences are well known, but they are also probably too simplistic to be fully true—for example, the Korean emphasis on exams, scores, extremely high stakes, and the sense of a young person's destiny hanging on success or failure on a test. Stories of Korean mothers who go into lockdown or take to bed because of

"Students should push themselves to seek opportunities to learn to do what makes them uncomfortable—whether it is speaking in public or writing."[15]

distress over a child's exams—are these just tall tales? I may be a too soft American, but I believe that serious love of learning should not be associated with childhood fear. These days, whether it's kindergarten, high school, or law school, educators like me think of learning as fun, and we want to instill a sense of excitement and wonder in the process of learning. I am reasonably sure, though, that Korean children know their multiplication tables and can spell sooner and better than American children of the same age. It is hard for me to say with confidence that one is objectively preferable, but as a result of the cultural influence I've had growing up in the U.S., I know which I would choose for my own children and my students and it's not even close.

I love students who come prepared to play the game. Students who are willing to try on different new possibilities and risks, take a break from their assumptions, be uncomfortable, be wrong, and roll with curveballs thrown at them. I have had all kinds of Korean students. Apart from the results of the Korean cultural tendency to socialize children in the family away from developing their speaking and argumentation skills, I have not noticed pronounced group characteristics in Korean students. As a teacher, I admit I actually don't think about whether my students are Korean. They are just my students, and I try to help them forge their paths as individuals.

Last year, I had the chance to write a series of columns for Korean readers in *Donga Ilbo* on issues arising out of my reflections on American law and legal education. As I wrote, I wondered of course whether my columns as an American law professor would strike Korean readers as relevant to the context of Korean society. I was gratified with pleasant surprise that there was indeed much connection and resonance there, even though my writing came out of the study of law and society in the United States. It was writing about an American context I knew well through my study and experience, and it thrilled me to able to communicate with Korean readers through ideas that could translate and relate to a culture and society I came from but do not know thoroughly.

I am Korean American, and I am hesitant to pronounce on Korean social and legal issues as I am sometimes asked to do. Korea is not my area of expertise in my scholarly life. I am not qualified to evaluate, diagnose, and judge its ills, and I think it is good to be reticent with respect to things one does not know. I have for example written about Comfort Women, but I did so to explain a point of American law in the context of a federal lawsuit with which I had good familiarity. Years lie ahead, though, in which I hope to engage in a deeper way with Korea, through learning, writing, and ideas that necessarily implicate cross-cultural reflections and translations.

When I was asked to write this autobiography for Korean readers, I became excited about the idea of telling one immigrant's story. What I didn't feel able to do, though, is to assume an authoritative voice instructing Korean readers on how to live and raise successful children. That is not what this book is for. I am unable to do more now than to tell my own story and to hope that it resonates for Koreans. It is difficult for me to write didactically—it is not my way. I apologize for that. But not unaware that some readers will desire some lessons to emerge from the story I've told, I will mention a few principles and observations in closing.

During a visit in Seoul last year, I had the chance to speak to audiences of students at several schools including my father's and mother's *almae matres*, Seoul National University and Ewha Woman's University. Distinguished members of the Korean legal community were good enough to arrange for me to meet with the Chief Justice of the Constitutional Court of Korea and with the Korean Minister of Justice. To my surprise, my visit to Seoul garnered the interest of fans and the attention of the Korean media. During the conversations, I was repeatedly asked if I knew the expression, *um chin tal*, and why I was called that name. I did not.

The expression was explained to me as follows: literally meaning "mother's friend's daughter," it refers to that paradigmatic other girl who is so exemplary in being talented, pretty, and smart that one's mom keeps talking about how perfect she is.

Being told of this meaning, I admit I was taken aback and rather horrified. While I appreciated the compliment, I could not relish this moniker, *um chin tal*. It is very annoying when one's mom keeps talking about her friend's perfect daughter and holding her up as some kind of model or wish. I myself have hoped that my mom would give it a rest and just leave her friends' daughters out of it. And the implicit comparison embedded within a mother's repetitive discourse of that nature can be alienating and hurtful.

I am the mother of two children, so my reaction is also influenced by that role. Children do not need to hear their mom go on about how perfect some other kid is, with an unspoken idea of who is more worthy of admiration. They need to have their mom affirm and cultivate their passions, interests, and pursuits. They should grow feeling loved and treasured for who they are rather than for appearing talented, pretty, and smart to their own mother or their mother's friends.

The idea of being tagged with a rhetorical label that represents how your mother compares you to other children by remarking how perfect they are caused me to wince with recognition. It made me want to say a thing or two to these hypothetical moms and children as soon as possible. It also made me want to write this book and tell my story.

I hope that if anything has come across in my story, it is the embracing of imperfection that growing up demands. The most precious aspect of my journey has been increasing freedom—to think, work, love, and play. It is impossible to feel free if you are trying to be perfect. It hurts! The discipline of working on something I love is rewarding. But it is not for being perfect. I cannot do it. Neither do I want that for my children.

I am not a perfect mother. I am not the best mother around. I'm just good enough. It goes without saying that I am not raising my children with the full-time attention my mother devoted to raising me. I am a full-time law professor. Like all women who have made huge commitments to their careers, I am constantly questioned how I manage to "*balance work and life*." It might even be the most frequent question I am asked.

The answer is that I don't. Work and life are not opposed poles that I strive to "balance." The notion of engaging in such a balancing act appears absurd to me. I live in my work and work in my life. Work and play go together. Work often feels like play. The joy my children give me is indescribable. And I can barely imagine happiness without my work.

My children talk to me about my research projects and writing as eagerly as I engage their emerging interests and pursuits.

"So, mommy, what's going on in your work these days?" they ask.

I tell them. It may mean explaining to them the criminal justice process from bail to jail, why the state punishes people for wrongdoing, arguments for and against the death penalty, how the Supreme Court recognized abortion as a constitutional right, or why we have copyright law.

I read books with my children, especially books I loved as a child. We have fun discovering new ideas and places together. I try to take them on travels and adventures whenever possible, as I consider those more important for children than their perfect attendance at school. We discuss what is happening in the world, in the country, in our schools and communities. I try to listen for their passions and to nurture them. We laugh and laugh and laugh. Often I am away working, and they are busy having fun with others—teachers, family members, caregivers, and friends. Sometimes they want me with them more. Sometimes I want to be with them but choose to work instead.

None of this feels like that proverbial balance. It is work in life, life in work. There is no formula here, just daily life with its pursuits, joys, pains, and disappointments. It is so imperfect. We get up the next day and begin again.

Often one hears talk about whether women can "have it all," as if that is a reasonable aspiration, hope, or even entitlement. This discourse of "having it all" is false to the extent that it implies that women might one day have something that men have. Nobody—man or woman—can "have it all." If you wish to engage in a professional pursuit at the highest level and be stellar at it, guess what, you will not to be able to be a full time or even half time parent—mom or dad—that is, without setting yourself up for a crisis that destroys your health, and what good would that do. You can most certainly be a loving parent who gives plenty of care to your children, but the time you spend with them will be very limited. That is the truth.

People often ask how I manage my time while being so busy. Each day is different. There are teaching days, in which mostly I prepare for teaching, teach, and see students. There are research and writing days, in which I park myself at my desk in my office at school or at home, and write for a while and read for a while. There are punctuations for meetings, workshops, and lunches with colleagues. There might be work-related dinners or dinners with friends. Sometimes there are trips for lectures or conferences. I endeavor to move my body at least every other day—I do pilates, yoga, or tennis. In the early evenings I am with my children for supper, books, bath, and bedtime. After they go to bed, I do some administrative and household tasks for an hour or two.

But all this sounds much simpler than it feels. Usually I lurch through the weeks and months wishing for Friday evening and summer to arrive so I can breathe. Breathing means more freedom and space to write, play, catch up with friends, spend long periods with my children, and cook meals. I always resolve to create consistent routines and simplify, simplify, simplify. The manageability of my schedule is more of an aspiration than reality. No matter what, I always try to take time to put lovely fresh flowers in a vase where I can see them as I work. Peonies are my favorite.

We all have to make choices about how to configure our lives—hopefully choices that reflect our values, desires, and preferences—allocate our time accordingly, and live with those choices. Yes, the professions should evolve to be increasingly friendlier to workers with children and to allow more work schedule flexibility. But that cannot really solve the basic issue, which is that there are no shortcuts when attempting to be excellent at something–it takes the investment of much time every day, week, month, year spent doing that thing. Whether it is scholarship, science, art, or parenting, the undeniable reality is that a staggering amount of time is required for men or women to do something at a very high level(so it had better be something you really like if this is your goal). And this will be true even if society is reformed to make it more comfortable for women and men both to work and to parent.

"There should be clear rewards for meeting goals. I sometimes even get myself a bunch of beautiful flowers."

Epilogue

Find What You Love to Do

We cannot all be Sarah Chang or Yu-Na Kim. So what? For most of us, the point of a pursuit is to gain rich knowledge and experience from which we can draw reward and pleasure for a long life. Music, for example, is among the greatest human inventions and gifts. If people stopped learning music when they realized they couldn't be Yo-Yo Ma, a lot of people in the world would needlessly stop developing what could be an incredible source of meaning in their lives.

I regret not having continued to dance. I'm still sad about it. It was a painful loss. More than half my life has gone by since that happened. Of course there are much worse things that can happen in life. But I would not snuff out a child's passion. The most likely result if I had continued of course is that I would have given up that particular dream eventually like many of my friends, because of injury or not being good enough. Had I actually become a professional dancer, the career would have been short. I would be in a second sequential career now. Maybe I would even be finishing law school and starting a legal academic career! I'm very fortunate to have found work I love so much. I love the life I have. I don't take that for granted. But nothing in this story makes me think it is a good idea to stand in the way of a child who is intensely self-propelled toward a particular creative endeavor. A child's passion is a very precious thing to be nurtured and treasured.

I hope for young people to have opportunities to discover and pursue what they love—the ideas, activities, passions, and thoughts that make them fully human. They should follow their passions, not a preset track that is expected of them. We should not all do the same things. We should use our freedom to grow in diverse ways. There are so many different possible paths to a good life. What are education, teaching, and parenting for if not to open up those possibilities of freedom?

My advice to students is to listen and be open to what you find fun and engaging. If something makes you excited to wake up in the morning, do that thing. Some parents will ask, what if my child is only excited to watch movies or play ball? Those are passions. I find it much less important what precisely the passion is than that there be passion. Does that mean the child is necessarily going to become a movie producer or ballplayer? Maybe or maybe not, but the experience of a passionate endeavor can be a template that enables people to be open to cultivating the tendencies and skills that can fulfill them in their later lives.

Parents can create opportunities for their children, but they cannot make children do things. Let children lead with their interests and then see them fly. I treasure the staggering gifts my parents have given me. I try to appreciate them not as debts, burdens, or duties, but rather as acts of setting me free.

Whatever the path, conflict and failure are not the end of the world. I hope the willingness to take risks will remain even when fear of conflict or failure creeps in. If you fail at something, don't walk away. When it feels impossibly difficult, take one small step and then another. Taking risks might make you do things that go against expectations. Letting fear or shame drive you makes it impossible to succeed.

Fear and shame at my own incompetence pervaded my

psyche as a young child with no English in an American classroom. This is a common experience of immigrants. As a child, surviving each day of school was an ordeal. But by necessity I confronted the multilingual and polyvalent nature of our lives. We can have fluency in cultures as well as in languages. The linguistic alienation that immigration produced for me became the template for the repeated process of moving from terrified incomprehension to mastery of particular tools needed to function in different social and institutional contexts.

It was important in the midst of navigating all this to develop an inner life from which to draw comfort—a light inside for looking out at the world. The hours I have spent since my childhood just daydreaming is staggering. And of course there were books then and there are books now. When I am tempted to feel that I am lazy and uncool because all I really want to do is sit at home and read, I comfort myself with yet another book, and remember Marcel Proust's remark: "There are perhaps no days of our childhood we lived so fully as those we believe we left without having lived them, those we spent with a favorite book." That favorite for me is Proust's *A la recherche du temps perdu(In Search of Lost Time).*

Since the heart of my professional life involves reading and research, I like to try to distinguish between books I read for work and books I read for pure pleasure—but of course they are inevitably intermingled. For some periods even today, I impose a rule that I can only read books for pleasure, and nothing related to my work if possible. With books I read for pleasure—fiction, nonfiction, poetry—I don't try to approach it as study. I love to reinhabit the wonder of the child reading, hoping I won't end up awake all night in a trance glued to the book, but also wanting desperately to do so.

For many people like me, the nourishment of reading and thinking leads to the desire to write. The habit of producing, of wanting to make things, is like the need for food. Going without for any length of time I can feel starved. But I struggled with writer's block for a long time. It is one of the mysteries of my intellectual development that I would love to unlock—how does one get out of that prison of feeling frozen, in writing and in life? I have tried to adopt humble and manageable goals for each day. My writer's block came from intimidation at the perceived enormity of what I needed to do. So I tried to cut down expectations. I began with a small goal of 250 words a day and moved up the word goal gradually day by day. I don't think I've ever written more than 2,000 words a day. But whatever the goal, I set it in advance, and try not to change it mid-way. If I meet the goal, I stop even if there are still hours left in the day to work even more. That means I get to reward myself when I am done—playing with my children, going out to dinner, reading a novel, going to a concert, or watching a movie. Work should not be allowed to expand to fill all the time you have. There should be clear rewards for meeting goals. I sometimes even get myself a bunch of beautiful flowers when I meet a writing goal.

There is no way to improve one's writing other than just doing a lot of writing over time and reading a lot of good writers. I like to read writing that is clear and accessible. Whatever stylish flourishes there may be in a person's writing, what is most appealing to me as a reader is a simple transparency that enables access to the depth and complexity of ideas. I am trying hard to be clearer in my writing.

I cannot claim to have accumulated great wisdom, but I have some aspirations for how I want to live.

I aspire to understand better the ideas and concepts through which we govern ourselves through law. To produce knowledge of the effects and meanings the law has in our lives.

I aspire to participate in making education a noble and vital path where one can freely think and speak the truth. To give to institutions and communities that have given me so much. To give to students abundantly what my teachers gave me.

I aspire to nurture the potential of young people so they can know more and go farther than my generation. To help students develop their voices and foster in them excellence and integrity. To enable them to unlock their creativity and wonder in the world of ideas. To urge them never to forget the humanity of those around them and those whom they do not know.

I aspire to be around people I love and share things that give joy. To be a loyal and compassionate friend in painful or tragic times. To allow friends to help me. To show up even when life feels urgently busy. To keep my friends close to me throughout our lives.

I aspire to live simply. To pursue work I love to do. To set achievable goals. To get plenty of sleep. To engage in activities that make me wake up excited to tackle them. To try new things. To embrace imperfection.

Finally, I aspire to have fun. To work hard and play hard. To make work into play. To laugh with others as often as possible.

To laugh at myself. Fun is infectious. It makes everything worth the trouble. I really can't do without it and neither should you. So ask yourself what is intensely fun for you and arrange to do that if you possibly can.

Acknowledgments

I am grateful for the contributions of those who helped me in producing this book. They include my editors at Bookhouse, Andrew Wylie and James Pullen at the Wylie Agency, Alex Lee at the Milkwood Agency, Neil Brenner, Annabel Chang, Noah Feldman, Amy Finkelstein, Jacob Gersen, Scott Hemphill, Janet Katz, David Korn, Alyssa Lary, Anthony Mariano, Hee Seok Shin, Song Nam Suk, Chang Ho Suk, Terry Teachout, and Sunshine Yin. I am also grateful to Dean Martha Minow, and to colleagues and friends whose conversation over the years made this writing possible. Any mistakes are my own. The MacDowell Colony allowed me to finish the manuscript in a charmed place, with quiet nourishment and remarkable company.

Sources

01. 「The House was Quiet and the World was Calm」, Wallace Stevens, *The Collected Poems of Wallace Stevens*, Alfred a Knopf Inc, 1954; 2008.

02. 「Among School Children」, W. B. Yeats, *The Collected Works of W. B. Yeats Vol. 1*, Scribner, 1997.

03. 「The Lake Isle of Innisfree」, W. B. Yeats, *The Collected Works of W. B. Yeats Vol. 1*, Scribner, 1997.

04. 「Metaphors」, Sylvia Plath, *The Collected Poems*, Buccaneer Books, 1998.

05. 「In Broken Images」, Robert Graves, *The Complete Poems Vol. 1*, Carcanet Pr, 2001.

06. 「At North Farm」, John Ashbery, *John Ashbery: Collected Poems 1956-1987*, Library of America; First Edition, 2008.

07. 「On First Looking into Chapman's Homer」, John Keats, *The Complete Poems of John Keats*, Modern Library; Modern Library Edition edition, 1994.

08. 「Correspondences」, Charles Baudelaire, *Les Fleurs du Mal*, Gallimard, 1999.

09. 「La vie anterieure」, Charles Baudelaire, *Les Fleurs du Mal*, Gallimard, 1999.

* The photographs reproduced in this book are reprinted by permission of their respective copyright owners.

10. P 212_《*DongA Ilbo*》 12. Dec. 2010.

11. P 215_《*Joongang Ilbo*》 10. Dec. 2011.

12. P 216_《*Yonhapnews*》 05. Dec. 2011.

13. P 219_《*Yonhapnews*》 14. Jan. 2011.

14. P 227_《*Yonhapnews*》 01. Dec. 2011.

15. P 245_《*The Korea Economic Daily*》 14. Nov. 2010.

* Some material in this book is adapted from Jeannie Suk's previously published writing in.

The Trajectory of Trauma: Bodies and Minds of Abortion Discourse,
110 Columbia Law Review 1193, 2010.

At Home in the Law; How the Domestic Violence Revolution Is Transforming Privacy, Yale University Press, 2009.

The Law, Culture & Economics of Fashion, 61 Stanford Law Review 1147
(with C. Scott Hemphill), 2009.

A Light Inside by Jeannie Suk

This edition published by arrangement with Jeannie Suk c/o The Wylie Agency (UK) through Milkwood Agency.

First Printing date	18 Feb. 2013
First Publication date	26 Feb. 2013

Written by Jeannie Suk

Publisher	Jeongsoon Kim
Editor	Seonheui Lee
Designer	Jinyoung Kim
Marketer	Bomi Kim, Jungjin Lim, Seonkyung Jeon

Published by Bookhouse Publishers, Co. Ltd.

Address	6F, Sunjin bldg., 395-4, Seogyo-dong, Mapo-Gu, Seoul, 121-840 KOREA
E-mail	editor@bookhouse.co.kr
Homepage	www.bookhouse.co.kr
Tel	+82-2-3144-3123
Fax	+82-2-3144-3121

ISBN 978-89-5605-632-6 13740
978-89-5605-619-7 03810(set)

Printed and bound in Korea.